MANDINKO

The Ethnography of a West African Holy Land

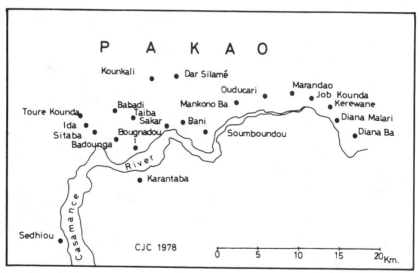

CJC 1978

MANDINKO
The Ethnography of a West African Holy Land

By

MATT SCHAFFER

with
ethnobotany and cartography
by
CHRISTINE COOPER

WAVELAND

PRESS, INC.

Prospect Heights, Illinois

For information about this book, write or call:
Waveland Press, Inc.
P.O. Box 400
Prospect Heights, Illinois 60070
(708) 634-0081

For Grayson and Ethan

About the Authors

Matt Schaffer is President of D.M. Schaffer Corporation, an investment banking firm specializing in mergers and acquisitions. In the private sector, he also has been director of countertrade at Sears World Trade and a consultant in the banking practice of McKinsey & Company. In government, he was appointed during the Carter Administration to be both assistant to the secretary of defense and, later, senior vice president for policy of the United States Export-Import Bank. During the Carter campaign of 1976, he was a coordinator for foreign policy and defense. In college he concentrated on French and African Studies. He received his B.A. from Yale in French in 1970 and was a Scholar of the House, writing a thesis on French African literature. He won a Rhodes Scholarship in 1971 and received his Ph.D. in Social Anthropology in 1976 from Oxford University.

Matt's wife, Christine Cooper, grew up in Massachusetts and attended the Buxton School in Williamstown. She studied anthropology at the University of Michigan, as well as at Oxford in England, and received her B.A. with distinction from Michigan in 1973. The collection of dried plant specimens that she and Matt collected with the Mandinko is now in the Oxford Herbarium. She was employed in the harpsichord workshops of David Rubio in Oxford and Frank Hubbard in Waltham, Massachusetts. She currently manages real estate investments and enjoys skiing and gardening. Christine and Matt were married in Oxford and have two sons, Ethan and Grayson. They live in Rockville, Maryland.

Acknowledgments

The field research for this study was made possible by financial support from the Rhodes Trust and by two grants from The National Geographic Society, Washington, D.C. We are most grateful for the assistance of numerous Senegalese. They include staff members of I.F.A.N. (l'Institut Fondamental d'Afrique Noire) at the University of Dakar and the librarians of the Senegalese National Archives. In particular, we would like to thank Kaoussou Sambou, a botanist at I.F.A.N., for his identification of plants and transcription of tapes. We appreciate the assistance of Mbemba Sagnan, a *lycée* student who helped us conduct demographic surveys of Mankono Ba and Soumboundou during the summer of 1974. We are also indebted to Bouly Dramé, the Mandinka civil servant whom we met at the London Manding Conference in 1972 and who directed us to the Pakao area of southern Senegal. We are grateful for the hospitality of Al Giannini, James Mayer, and Jim Sharp, all members of the U.S. Peace Corps who served in southern Senegal. We also value the help of Sally and Jim Blanford, U.S. Foreign Service, during our research in Dakar. Bruce McElfresh, Picture Editor of *National Geographic* magazine, provided useful instruction in photography and photographic editing. We also appreciate the loyal support of Dr. Edwin W. Snider, Secretary of the Committee for Research and Exploration at National Geographic. We owe a special debt of gratitude to many friends and colleagues in Great Britain. Matt's D.Phil. supervisor at Oxford, Rodney Needham, offered insight, encouragement, and discipline without which this work would not have come to fruition. We also want to thank Anthony Boyce, Frank White, Sir Edgar Williams, Sir Richard Southern, Edwin Ardener, and Godfry Lienhart, all of Oxford; David Dalby, Director of the International African Institute, and Winifred Dalby; and the librarians of Rhodes House, the Royal Anthropological Institute, the School of Oriental and African Studies, and the Institute of Social Anthropology.

MATT SCHAFFER
CHRISTINE COOPER

Preface, 1987

Friends and students have often asked if fieldwork was frightening or dangerous. I down-played this aspect in the first edition, preferring to focus as much as possible on Mandinka ethnography. Truth is, there were many frightful moments, but we fared well by being both very careful and lucky. Some of the most difficult times occurred away from the relative safety of a densely populated village.

While on bicycle trips between villages more than ten miles apart, I was twice nearly bitten by a black spitting cobra that reared up with hood flared, practically standing on its tail, inches from my foot as I pedaled quickly by. In both cases, the snakes decided to flee rather than to strike. The Mandinko of Dar Silamé and Karantaba especially appreciated my description of the near misses because the black cobra (*beeda*) is the totem (*tano*) of the Dramé clan which provides the chiefs of both villages. Dramé was the clan name given me. As with many tribal peoples, a clansman is never supposed to harm or kill his totem. In this case, I was fortunate that the respect turned out to be mutual, and I was pleased in a way to have at last seen my dangerous totem.

On another occasion near Karantaba while collecting plant medicine with Lan Soli Bantanjao, the latter actually did step on a snake more than six feet long with his bare foot. Scarcely two feet in front of me he leaped back nimbly, cut a staff quickly and killed the snake. He said this type of boa had killed goats, sheep and even children.

During the first months of fieldwork in 1972 and into 1974, the revolution in Guinea Bissau was still going on about twenty-five miles away. It was not unusual to hear distant shelling or bombing, especially at night when the village grew quieter. Although we heard of armed soldiers making pilgrimages to the mosque of Karantaba, we fortunately never saw any, except on one occasion.[1]

---

[1] Refugees from Guinea Bissau did make their way into Southern Senegal. Several Manjak villages of roughly fifty people each were established by refugees who had fled the fighting in the early 1970's. Some land disputes were beginning to arise with the much larger Mandinka villages. Although the Manjak were tolerated, they were not allowed to live in Pakao villages.

On a day when the war was allegedly over and independence was supposed to occur, I saw a huge column of dust while riding my bicycle on the one dirt road bisecting Pakao. It was a tank coming toward me straight down the road at a surprisingly high speed. There was a brief sickening moment as I peered down the barrels of a cannon and machine gun, not knowing whose tank this was (Senegalese, Portuguese, Guinea Bissau rebels), why it was going so fast or whether its driver and machine gunner would want to take a little target practice on me with no witnesses around. Trying to take one small step to improve the odds, I nearly tore the handle bars off that bike trying to get away from the road and out of the way. I never did find out the identity of that tank.

In Dar Silamé, the villagers laughed with real empathy when I told of walking in alone from Sakar after a heavy rain with a cumbersome backpack, noticing very fresh cat tracks deeply imprinted in the wet sand midway between the villages. Too exhausted to turn back, I decided to press ahead, unavoidably following the tracks, probably of a large leopard, for a mile. When the tracks finally turned from the dirt road, I nervously plodded past praying that the beast had wandered into the jungle and was not watching me.

Trips in the narrow, shallow dugout canoes were always cause for concern. The most harrowing trip involved trying to get our bicycles and ourselves across the Casamance River from Karantaba at a point more than a mile wide. Putting the bikes across the boat, we nervously shifted our weight to counterbalance movements of the paddle. The sides of the canoe were about an inch above the water, and I had a feeling the waterlogged boat would sink if it capsized.

While I most often ran into difficulty while travelling, living in a Mandinka village was hardly routine. During a terrible nightmare in Karantaba, I dreamed of a rat eating my head and woke up from the shock. Taking the flashlight which was always kept under my pillow, I pulled my head away from the mosquito netting and saw, spread-eagled on the net, a large rat of two or three pounds. I felt my head and realized it had been nibbling at my hair sticking through the mosquito netting as I inadvertently pushed against it. What does one do in such a ridiculous situation? I balled up my fist and hit the rat with a crushing blow, feeling its rather heavy weight against my fist, and sent it smashing into the wall on the other side of the hut. The Mandinko I stayed with in Karantaba enjoyed that story because they often interpret dreams or use them to seek some deeper understanding of events.

When a small filling fell out of my tooth in Karantaba causing excruciating pain, it was cause for a major misadventure compared with a simple trip to the dentist back home. I did not want to take a week and return to Dakar the capital. Hoping against hope to find a dentist, I decided to try Ziguinchor, the provincial capital. The journey took one and a half days, beginning with a ten-mile bicycle ride to Sandiniéri and a dugout canoe trip to Sédhiou, where I was finally able to catch a bush taxi to Ziguinchor by way of two ferries.

At the hospital, I was overjoyed to hear that, in fact, a French military dentist was available, the only one in Senegal south of the Casamance River. He was at home. I nervously rang the doorbell. The most unintelligible moan came gurgling from a room inside, "Alloooooo." When the doctor answered the door five minutes later, he looked half-dead, covered like a mummy in bandages with blood and stitches all over him. Speaking painfully slowly, he told about an automobile accident that nearly killed him the day before. Seeing that I too was in pain, he graciously offered to help.

His dental chair looked more like the electric chair with its huge arm rests and stiff, high back. He ominously raised his mechanical drill. I asked plaintively, "Do you have Novocaine?" He answered predictably, "Of course not. You must be joking. My precious one bottle must be saved for major surgery." Letting him grind away, I gripped the huge chair as hard as possible, now understanding the purpose of the large arm rests. The cure was almost as bad as the problem. At last, the pain was gone, and I have always been grateful to that courageous doctor.

Fortunately, we were never sick in a village but were nearly always hungry, despite a few extra tins of tuna and sardines. During the worst part of the drought in 1972, we came out of Dar Silamé together for the first time and returned to Sédhiou, in all candor nearly starving. The local Lebanese merchant longing, we later discovered, for the rare company of white people, one night invited Christine and me to a sumptuous feast that we have never forgotten. After serving home-grown lamb and vegetables, he offered imported French butter, wine and Grand-Marnier, topping the dinner off with a flaming crêpe-suzette. He spoke fluent Mandinko but used it to browbeat and criticize his Mandinka servants during the meal. The setting was in a beautiful courtyard behind his store, under a huge Mango tree and next to his swimming pool. To complete the meal, he smoked a cigar and coolly asked that his rifle be brought to him. Pushing back from the table, while still seated, he casually shot bats from his Mango tree with the eye of an expert marksman. Suddenly, a summer squall blew up within seconds, pounding rain through the tree and sending us scrambling from the dinner table. He graciously offered us a room with mosquito screens and clean sheets, as well as a soft bed. I gave up trying to resolve the contradictions and instead listened to the delicious rain, falling asleep in heavenly bliss. Later nights in the field were never so good, and during one break, I went sleepless with the usual bad crop of bedbugs in the Peace Corps house, finding myself covered in the morning with bloody marks from their bites. One learns fast from the Mandinko to arrive for a visit early enough in the hot day to put the mattress out into the sun to drive off the bedbugs.

The Peace Corps house in Sédhiou, where I stayed for one- or two-day visits a few times during fieldwork, had its own special problems. One night I had decided to sleep on the porch to get some relief from the oppressive heat. Something told me to wake up and move back inside. Late that night, a blood-red, bark-masked figure called a *kangkurao* woke me up with its shrieking outside. With the two machetes it traditionally carries, it furiously slashed the concrete where I had slept, all the while making a terrible clanging noise.

A lone *kangkurao* is one of the most dangerous forces to the Mandinko because there is no escorting group of youths to control it. This man-made demon-spirit, or *gino*, represented a sort of tentative truce between the world of men, where control was possible, and the dangerous world of demon-spirits, where control was not always possible. To the Mandinko, there was a kind of spiritual equilibrium in a dangerous world with demon-spirits *(gino)* and cannibal-witches *(bwa)* offset by *marabouts* with their medicinal charms and wizards ("wide-heads" or *kumfanunte*) with their eerie ability to spot these spirits or witches in whatever form they might take.

Unlike ourselves, the Mandinko felt grave danger where the magical potential for harm was far greater than any sense of physical threat. A curious incident illustrates this point.

One morning, in the fields north of Dar Silamé, I saw my host Wandifa Cissé's sons throwing limes at their cattle. Wondering whether this was some new ritual or just plain hooliganism, I asked why. They explained that the villagers of Dar Silamé including their father were greatly disturbed by the unexplained death of several cattle thought to have been killed by an evil "demon-spirit" *(gino)*. To protect them, every animal had a lime[2] thrown against it once each morning and a string *grigri* or charm blessed by a *marabout* or Islamic priest tied around the base of its tail. Of course, many Mandinko themselves wore additional *grigris* during this time of increased danger.

Anthropologists often wonder what impression they make on villagers with the former's hard struggle in the context of a different culture set against possible local envy of their more readily available food and medicine. When Mamadou Cissé, of my host hamlet in Dar Silamé, got to know me well, he teased me with two nicknames. One was *nyo bano*, "millet thief" (translation: busybody). The other was perhaps even more colorful, *sibijendibengo*, "the shadow of the *sibo*," a tall tree that casts a long shadow (i.e., someone who asks too many questions).

A sense of humor was terribly important because the Mandinko viewed the ability to exchange teasing as synonymous with good relations. In Soumboundou, I sometimes relaxed by talking to my host chief Toumany Jeta Camera about Mungo Park (the Scottish explorer who travelled among the Mandinko in the late eighteenth and early nineteenth centuries), even reading aloud to him from Mungo Park's *Travels* and translating from English to Mandinko. Toumany picked up on this when I later returned to Soumboundou, offering me some praise that I really appreciated: "You are stronger than Mungo Park. You took the trouble of staying longer in the same place. You even survived our deplorable food situation. We do not have enough food, and it often tastes terrible." An anthropologist who visits Soumboundou and believes he or she has heard an oral history of Mungo Park's actual journey will be wrong. For all I know, Mungo Park is probably intermingled with the story of Alex Haley's *Roots*, which I also told Toumany about. Finally, before feeling too good about Toumany's compliment, I must remember that he is from a long line of *fino*

---

[2]The lime was also used in several medicinal potions for humans.

praise-singers with an incurable tendency to use exaggerated praise and elaboration.

When the first book was published, I did not like the idea that copies would be unavailable to Mandinko. The assignments director, Bud Miles at McKinsey & Company, gave me a chance to resolve this problem. With his ever keen awareness of the background of his business consultants, he assigned me to the African correspondent banking study for a New York money center bank. The first stop for me was Banjul in the Gambia in January, 1981, several years after the two field trips of 1972 and 1974-75.

The Mandinka driver from the airport had a new Peugeot and agreed to let me hire him for a journey of some two hundred miles to Dar Silamé. On the way from the airport, he and I were both amazed that my Mandinko was still fluent and that I could identify nearly all the trees and bushes we passed. This was basic knowledge for a villager. I suppose the driver was really a city Mandinko. I discovered pleasantly that the Mandinko in coastal Banjul had only the slightest differences in accent and that I could speak to both the vendors in the market and the Mandinka governor of the central bank.

The trip back to Dar Silamé was memorable. Somehow, the driver got his car around the huge car-sized potholes on the path/road from Sakar to Dar Silamé. (Just before Sakar, he was so mad that he stopped the car, got out, and jumped up and down on the dirt road, saying that I had tricked him, that Dar Silamé was farther than I promised.)

In Dar Silamé, I found the *marabout* Omar Sylla, whose picture is on the book's cover, sitting on the bamboo platform of Sylla hamlet reading from his Koran to the faithful exactly as he was doing nine years earlier when Christine took the picture. Omar and the others laughed. Of course he should be on the cover. Of course he should be doing the same thing. After receiving his copy, he gave me many *dua* or Islamic blessings. I found my host Wandifa Cissé at the mosque and his wife Sanjiba Drame at their home. They were immensely pleased to receive copies of the book and somewhat amazed that I had actually returned. I reminded Sanjiba that she had cried years before when told I was leaving, that she had said I would never return. Later we spent hours talking into the mild evening with the others of Cissé hamlet and the village, as we had done so many nights before. To Mamadou Cissé, I could say that "the millet thief" and "the shadow of the *sibo* tree" were not forgotten. Keba Dramé was travelling, so his copy was left with Wandifa, my host, and Keba's cross-cousin. Large crowds formed around the books as people looked at the pictures, many seeing pictures of themselves for the first time. There was amusement, laughter, perhaps joy. The yearly *harmattan* wind was blowing in from the Sahara in the north. It was incredibly hot and dusty at the height of the dry season, and I kept thinking, "God this is difficult; how could I have lived here so many months." My clothes were covered with dust. I practically choked breathing on dust. Then one more Mandinka night... mice scampering, bats darting and fluttering in the house awakened me as usual. Howling dog packs savagely roamed the village. The low distant calling of a hyena, almost cooing like a dove mingled with the early crowing of the roosters. The first piercing call for prayers at five a.m. gave way to a steady thumping as early rising women pounded their grain with mortar and pestle to begin the day.

In the morning, I stopped by to see the house of Fodé Ibrahima Dramé, who had welcomed us into the village on the very first day of fieldwork and had finally agreed to tell me the myth of the Islamic warrior Syllaba. His house and subhamlet were now in ruins after his death, and his family was relocated around the one precious incoming road, moving a few hundred yards closer to Sakar.

The first two weeks in Dar Silamé had been the toughest, waiting for Fodé to tell me the myth of Syllaba, waiting and waiting. Imagine quietly waiting two weeks, prodding, offering to leave, negotiating, worrying about getting ill just so an old man would tell me a story that was central to the way a people think about themselves. The virtues of patience that are not taught in graduate school were learned through experience.

Included below are some poems written when I lived with the Mandinko, as well as one written more recently.

Rockville, Maryland
June, 1987

From *Two Worlds*

Karantaba — June 26, 1974

We are trudging
Beneath our sweat
With the burden of foreknowledge
That we grant wherever we go
The right to haunt in dreams.
Behind our thoughts
Our bodies drag
Through hot exhaustion
Locked
Into the blindness of descent.
In the middle of the rainy season
There is no rain in this forest
Whose green outrageously deceives,
Whose great trees mock their fate,
And dust swells
Around swollen feet.
It is not the heavens
Opening up to thunder down,
But dilated pores
Pumping rage,
Cleaning house.
Muscles lug dead weight
And bones would break
Except for sheer stubbornness.
Into this bag of humanness
Strange air is sucked.
What breathes out
Is first of all relief,
Then shame
Before the few, empty seconds
Permit the concentration of vision

And the slowing of movement
Prior to the momentary opening of sight.
In this sharpened state
We shall meet
On one condition,
That foreigners leave.
For we have set ourselves
In this place
Not simply to learn
Or to write down
But to take it in
Before the something else
Whose design is in us
In the making.
If confidence to intake
This whatever does not fail
And we are drawn toward staying
Beyond the internal balance of our two worlds,
We shall up and leave anyway.
Being finished
Is necessary illusion,
Like hacking last furrows
Bent over with a homemade hoe
In parched earth
Because tomorrow it rains.
Being done
Is just clutching up one's hoe
And walking away
In the evening
To settle down
On home ground.

From *Two Worlds*

Karantaba — July 28, 1974

Shadowing the earth,
Damp dungeons
Well up in the sky.
Up from watery pits
Women drawing water
Glance.
Into dark holes
Their black buckets fall.
Cattle crowd the mud
To lick the spill.
Distant thunder cracks
Beneath the clouds
Where villages are shelled.
Dusk light flashes far away
With rumbling disconnected.
Air smells stale
As if breathed too long.
Night wind blots
Out all above
And closes in.
Drops are flung
In darkness
Against roofs of straw and tin.
Now a tantalizing mist.
Now a crop ripping dump.
Damn rain.

Karantaba — July 30, 1974

Last sleep.
Early rise.
Swift steel tool
Lifting stranger from friends
Beyond good-bye.
Weightless
Into primeval silence,
New morning thoughts arise
Merely forces among the forces
Of motions balanced.
Bound to a path
With a feeling of freedom.
Human baggage lashed
To the handicraft of blacksmiths.
Wrought sliver
Released through the peace
Of unhuman spaces.
Crossing river.
Changing village.
Bicycle stashed
In the bow of a dugout canoe.

The Drum
Bethesda, Maryland — 1985 to February, 1986

In the luckiest of lifetimes
There is a moment
That soars
Like the fullest crystalline moon in the blackest sky.
Its purity makes it last
In thought like the sweetest dream.
Despite the years
This one Mandinka night keeps coming back,
So simply moon-lit
And magically cool
With the driest desert air from the north.
The subtleties of moon-shadows
Stream across the village paths
Beneath gigantic trees.
Out of the soft darkness a drum
Begins to toll
With an easy ancient elegance
In the realm of the soul.
Uneven eternal structures of infinite appeal
Are pulling me
Through the heaven that is a sound across the field.
Forgetting past and future
In the fetal-like pleasure of such heartbeats
I am quickly walking toward the gathering of men and boys.
They sing and clap with lingering staccato to break
The sonorous bass drum rhythms
That slowly accelerate
As a power that lifts in time and space
And became for me
The finest memory of a place.
I suppose I can never return
Though I will tell you that on this night
They have given me the drumsticks
And told me to play.
It is a music so large
And irresistible
That I am easily blended in their singing
And taught to flee the world
Through the bodily rhythms of escape.
It is a song like a mother's kiss
That is always sung well
With a beat that tells
And is never missed.

Contents

Missera: The circumcision novices.

Missera: Inside the circumcision lodge, the lodge chief, Landing Dramé, issues the command for the novices to begin their breakfast around communal bowls of millet broth.

Dar Silamé: Sanjiba Dramé, the wife of our host, Wandifa Cissé, prepares the noon meal in her cook-house.

Introduction

This is a study about a West African people whose name has been widely popularized by Alex Haley in *Roots*. Because of Haley and others, the Mandinko[1] of the Gambia and southern Senegal (Senegambia) have received an almost mythical dimension, raising very serious and legitimate questions about them as a contemporary people. From the American perspective there is one question dominating all others. What is the relationship between slavery and the Mandinko? In the context of Haley's book *Roots* and the television series, it is really impossible to describe Mandinko life without at least a note on the issue. I do this before proceeding on to the main questions of the book: What is it like to do fieldwork among the Mandinko? How is their society organized? What do we know about how the society has changed over the years? One obvious change is that enforced slavery is no longer the fact of life that it was in previous centuries.

The very first Portuguese ships to reach black Africa captured slaves (Boulègue 1968:122–124). When Dinis Dias landed in 1444 on Cape Verde, the westernmost point in Africa, he imprisoned four men who came to meet the boat. By 1446 the Portuguese, under Alvar Ferandes, had voyaged a few hundred miles further south and reached the Gambia and the Casamance, two great rivers running through the heart of Mandinko country. The number of Mandinko who eventually became victims of the Atlantic slave trade will probably never be known accurately. Those original slave lists that do include tribal names were used somewhat indiscriminately by the traders and may have sometimes indicated geographic region rather than ethnic group. The historian Philip Curtin recognizes this difficulty (1969:184–185), and arrives at a very tentative projection of ethnic and regional percentages. In the quarter century 1526–1550, he projects that roughly 8 percent of the slaves taken from Africa (to Latin America and the Caribbean) were Mandinko, and that the Senegambia as a region provided about 38 percent (1975:13). Slaves were not transported to America until 1619. By the eighteenth century the Senegambia provided decreasing percentages, dropping to less than 1 percent of the African total by 1810 (Curtin 1969:221). It would therefore seem likely that by the time Alex Haley's ancestor was enslaved, other

---

[1] Both the singular and plural form of the noun is *Mandinko,* a term which thus refers either to a person or to the people. *Mandinka* is the adjective.

1

more southerly regions in Africa had become the principal suppliers in the overall slave trading network.

The Mandinko were not only victims of the slave trade, but perpetrators of it. They have a long history of owning and maintaining slaves. From the seventeenth through the nineteenth centuries there are several descriptions of the indigenous slave system.[2] Mandinka slaves are to be distinguished from the *slatees*, who were free black merchants specializing in the slave trade and who often had contacts with white traders (Park 1969:16). Slaves owned by the Mandinko were often either captured in battle or born into bondage. During his first trip through the Senegambia in 1795–1797, Mungo Park estimated that about three-fourths of the population were hereditary slaves (1969:16). It was also possible for a Mandinko to be sold by his or her fellow villagers as punishment for a serious crime. In the seventeenth century, Richard Jobson listed this practice for adultery (1968:67). In the eighteenth century, Francis Moore (1738:42) expanded the list to include murder and theft, and writing in 1799, Mungo Park (1969:227) added witchcraft. During the travels of Francis Moore from 1730–1735, the punishment of enslavement was reported to be quite common and was even meted out for offenses such as petty theft and accidental manslaughter (1738:42). In the late 1700s, Mungo Park described a more unusual cause for enslavement (1969:226). Responding to a severe drought in the Gambia region, many freemen voluntarily enslaved themselves to relatively well-off tribesmen so as not to perish from hunger.

In a good summary of sources, the historian Quinn (1972:15–16) points out that the Mandinko (and other West Africans) distinguished between slaves captured or purchased, and those born into villages where their slave families were established. Slaves in the first category were considered "little more than trade goods." Slaves in the second category had several rights and privileges, sometimes including the ability to purchase freedom. Hereditary slaves could be given Mandinka names at birth, and could not be sold or put to death without a public trial. These slaves could work some days each week for themselves, and on occasion became wealthier than their owners. Quinn also cites examples of slaves' holding highly responsible positions, as advisor to the king (in Wuli Kingdom), and as a collector of customs from European traders (in Niumi Kingdom).

While the British succeeded in suppressing the Atlantic slave trade out of the Gambia in the early 1800s,[3] the indigenous capture of slaves persisted throughout much of the nineteenth century, and a Mandinka slave caste system persists through the present day. The 1800s saw the outbreak of fierce sectarian wars between neighboring kingdoms, as well as *jihads* launched by Islamic Mandinko to convert their non-Muslim brethren forcibly. These wars resulted in the abduction of many slaves, often women and children (who were easier to control and convert), and persons from adjacent ethnic groups. The era of warfare was finally put down by the French colonial army with the massacre of Fodé Keba's forces in 1901 at the

[2] See, for example, Jobson 1623 and 1968:78–79; Moore 1738: 41–43; Park 1969 (and 1799) :220–228; Hecquard 1855:100 and 120.

[3] Leary (1969:79) notes that the British abolished slavery in 1808 and that France reached a similar decision in 1815. Some slaves nevertheless continued to be brought to shipping ports by clandestine routes. French purchasing of slaves is recorded at the Sédhiou Fort on the Casamance until 1848.

battle of Madina. It appears likely that the capture of slaves in battle had stopped by this time, if not some years before. However, commercial slave transactions among indigenous populations may have lasted a while longer. For example, a market existed on Carabane Island, near the mouth of the Casamance River, until 1902 (Leary 1969:79).

The modern slave caste in Pakao, the former Senegambian kingdom where Chris and I did fieldwork, is a legacy of the internal slave system of previous centuries. Its members are today found in all villages, and while they no longer work for their "owners," they must marry within the caste. The *jungo* or slave will be discussed in detail elsewhere in this book within the context of the two additional castes, *sula* (nobles) and *nyamalo* (artisans and praise-singers); the latter are sometimes also known as *griots*.[4]

Among today's hereditary castes, the stigma of being descended from a slave has caused most vestiges of the pretwentieth century slave system to be covered up. Yet there are reminders. A slave name such as Nomo is retained by a few women in Mankono Ba (Pakao), although men with these names have changed them. The ancestral village area of the Gitté slave family in Dar Silamé (Pakao) is known as Jongkundato, "the slave quarter." Legends are told about the capture of slaves in Mandinka jihads and wars of the nineteenth century. And it is still sometimes possible to hear a child teased with words that send it scrambling home: *Mba samba tubabo doo* ("I shall bring you to the land of the white man"). Mandinka informants in Pakao knew that some of their ancestors had been taken overseas by *tubabo* (white men). Yet the capture of slaves specifically by white traders was not a subject that turned up in the oral traditions I recorded. The occasional mention of slaves referred either to those owned by Mandinko or captured by them during internal wars. The most popular subjects of Mandinka legends were war heroes and the founders of villages.

Who are the Mandinko? Informants recount with considerable pride that their ancestors came from Manding. This is a local name for the ancient Mali empire, whose heartland lies in present-day Mali; indeed, the name *Mandinko* means "those from Manding." Teachers often cite ancient Mali as an example of a major black African civilization. At its height about 1300, this empire occupied much of the northern half of West Africa. The famous medieval university of Timbuctu was within its borders, and elsewhere in the empire mines yielded substantial quantities of gold. Arabic geographers have recorded that in 1324 the Emperor of Mali, Mansa Musa, caused a sensation during a pilgrimage through Egypt by distributing large amounts of gold among the populace. Fortunately, a very considerable body of Arabic accounts of Mali have been examined by Nehemia Levtzion (1973) and others, and a record of this empire is now more accessible.

Legend has it that the first Mandinka immigrants to the Gambia and Casamance River areas were warriors led by Tiramakhan Traoré. Tiramakhan is held to have been an important war chief of Sundjata, the legendary king who unified frag-

---

[4] I prefer "praise-singer" to the Senegalese French *griot* (pronounced *greo*). The Mandinko is *jalo* or *jeli*.

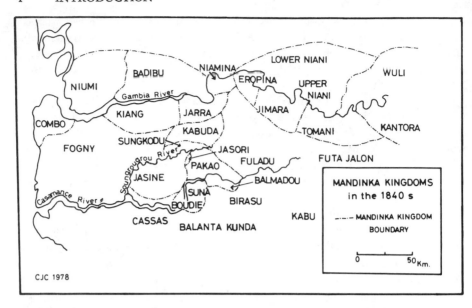

mented villages and founded the Mali empire sometime during the first half of the thirteenth century (see Levtzion 1973:61–62, 71, and 95).

From the thirteenth through the seventeenth centuries, the Mali empire expanded into the Senegambia, and more than twenty Mandinka kingdoms were founded along the Gambia and Casamance Rivers. Fifteenth-century Portuguese explorers reported that these kingdoms paid tribute to the emperor of Mali. Then, in the sixteenth century, the Mandinka empire of Kabu rose in importance. This empire, lying mostly in present-day Guinea Bissau, began as part of the larger Mali system, but at various times from the sixteenth through the eighteenth centuries exerted influence over the smaller Senegambian Mandinka kingdoms. The rise of Kabu was one signal that the old Mali empire had lost its importance and had been replaced by increasingly autonomous Senegambian kingdoms. During the nineteenth century, these were the kingdoms that were subjugated by the British in Gambia and the French in Senegal and incorporated into their two respective colonial systems.

It must already be obvious that the Senegambian Mandinko are too widespread to be studied extensively in one ethnography. Instead, I concentrated on one of the former kingdoms, named Pakao, although I have been able to make use of sources referring more generally to Senegambian Mandinko. Pakao (pronounced *Pakow*) is a twenty-four-village system where I lived for fifteen months during 1972 and 1974–1975. Three months were spent consulting colonial papers in the Senegalese National Archives in Dakar, and it took several additional months to consult books and unpublished papers about the Mandinko in British libraries.

Pakao lies on the upper reaches of the Casamance River in southern Senegal. It is about sixty miles south of the Gambia River and ninety miles southeast of Juffure, the village where Alex Haley claims ancestry. The Mandinka language of the former kingdoms along the Gambia and Casamance Rivers is virtually the same, with some differences in accent. The social institutions of Pakao are probably typical for the region, but I would not be surprised to hear of some variations and differences as additional fieldwork in other former kingdoms is pursued.

Pakao is unusual among these other areas in terms of the high degree of Islamic specialization among its people. Its self-concept is that of a Muslim holy land. This belief is based on a number of factors, including visits made by many foreign pilgrims from Gambia and other parts of Senegal. The prayers of interdiction uttered by Pakao *marabouts* are thought to have great power. A *marabout* (pronounced *marabu*) is a trained cleric who specializes in religious/magical functions; there are many such persons in every Pakao village. Locally, the mosques of Pakao are thought to be the oldest among the former Mandinka kingdoms.[5] In 1843–1844, Pakao was responsible for launching the first successful indigenous *jihad* in the region. A *jihad* is a Muslim holy war waged for the purposes of winning new converts, by force if necessary, and destroying nonbelievers if they are unwilling to accept Islam. By 1850, Pakao appears to have converted to Islam almost entirely, earlier than other Mandinka kingdoms in the area. This fact alone makes it a good community to examine the changes brought about by Islam as well as the durability of certain pre-Islamic customs.

Where do the Mandinko fit in the broader African context? The modern Mandinka village system is quite sedentary, with individual villages often having remained in place for two centuries or more. This kind of stability distinguishes the Mandinko from certain more mobile Fulani groups of the Sahel region and the Tuareg of the southern Sahara. The Mandinko are still great travelers, despite the permanence of their villages, and have a history of migration for purposes of conquest, trade, and religious proselytizing. Like many African peoples, the Mandinko own cattle. Their cattle, however, play only a peripheral economic role and are maintained largely for the prestige of owning them. Their place in Mandinka society thus contrasts dramatically with the system in several East African societies called "the cattle complex." In this system, common to Nilotic peoples such as the Nuer and Dinka, cattle are central to economic and ritual life. For example, cattle are used for bride wealth. The Mandinko also have a bride wealth system, but it is based on cash obtained from the sale of peanuts.

As Muslims, of course, the Mandinko share the religion of Islam with a great many peoples living roughly in a band stretching across Africa immediately south of the Sahara. There are nevertheless many different variations of Islam, depending on the ethnic group. One very pervasive Mandinka institution seems to contradict Islam's prohibition against graven images. This is a secret society organized around a mask-wearer (who adorns himself in a bark costume). Similar cults are reported for the Malinke of eastern Senegal, the Bambara of Mali, and certain other West African peoples related to the same Manding ethnic and cultural group.

---

[5] Weil says that the first mosque in the Gambia was not constructed until the latter half of the nineteenth century and that the second was not built until after World War II (1971:291). In 1850, Hecquard reported a small mosque in one Pakao village (1855:91). His travels in 1850–1851 confirm that Pakao was largely Muslim, while the Gambian kingdoms he visited were mostly non-Muslim.

Dar Silamé: Karamo Dabo and his son walk their cattle to a nearby field. Karamo was the last imam *of Kounkali village before its few remaining inhabitants disbanded and moved to Dar Silamé.*

1 / Fieldwork

There is an awkwardness to fieldwork that must be transcended and overcome. For example, the Mandinko talked about the circumcision of boys and girls as their most important ritual. They discussed circumcision secretly and fearfully, and made me think about it the same way. Here were Mandinko suggesting that the ritual removal of the foreskin and clitoris was central to their concept of social order and that it had to do with defining the relationship of men and women. How was I to study something that people did not like to talk about except to say that it was terribly important?

From the beginnning of our visit, Mandinka villagers speculated that a circumcision and seclusion would occur after a certain number of months or seasons. This did not happen until I was in my last month of fieldwork in Dar Silamé, when word came to me of a circumcision ceremony to be held in nearby Soumboundou. On December 27 (1974), I awakened at the first light of dawn and rode my bicycle the five miles to Soumboundou, pedaling as fast as possible over the hard path. Dancing had been going on all night. The chief, who had invited me to the circumcision several months previously, confirmed his invitation. As we approached the site east of the village, one man protested my presence. I was unlucky. He had become something of a racist during his years in the Senegalese Army, and there was nothing the chief could do about his objection. Dejected, I returned to the village and spent the day learning about the setting of the ritual and the building of the lodge, where the male novices would remain secluded for several weeks. I returned to Dar Silamé at dusk. Long into the night I discussed the misadventure in Soumboundou with the men of Cissé hamlet, where I lived. They told me what I wanted to hear and, I think, what they believed. The artisans and praise-singers of Soumboundou were unlike the nobles of Dar Silamé. They could be difficult and were not always to be trusted. The man who barred me from circumcision was said to be a little tyrant. He dominated Soumboundou and its chief, sometimes to the detriment of the community. (For instance, over the protest of villagers, he cut down a large tree, which fell the wrong way and demolished several houses, including his own.) He meddled in the affairs of other villages. Once, he led a squad of self-appointed vigilantes to Dar Silamé and forcibly abducted a Soumboundou youth who had taken refuge there. Suspected of stealing only a clock, the boy was savagely beaten, without any sort of inquest, and was then handed over to the authorities.

7

The next morning I discussed the problem of witnessing a circumcision ceremony with chief Fode Ibrahima Dramé. He was joined by another elder named Bakary Daffé, and the two men talked about the matter. They concluded that theoretically my presence at the ritual should not cause any problems and could be permitted. Bakary then turned to a problem of concern to him, and confided in the chief that he feared for his health. Bakary had tuberculosis, was blind in one eye and had such severe leprosy that several of his fingers and toes were missing. I said a long *dua*, a prayer mixing Arabic and Mandinko and asking Allah to heal his bodily ills. The old chief, who often pondered his own death, listened and smiled when Bakary replied appreciatively to me. "Omar, now you are a Mandinko," he said. Yet I was not a Mandinko; there was only so much I could learn and that was that.

On the way back to Cissé hamlet, I was stopped by Buté Sylla, who wanted to chat about my difficulty in Soumboundou the previous day. "Are you circumcised?" he suddenly asked. This was his way of consoling me. Assuming that I was not, he explained, "They will not let you witness the ritual unless you have been circumcised." Embarrassed, I had to admit to him that I was circumcised. Buté asked incredulously if white people circumcise their children. I nodded, realizing that he and other Mandinko had considered white people inferior to themselves for not having undergone the ritual.

Then, within a week, news broke that a boys' circumcision had been carried out in Missera. An invitation was extended for kinsmen in Dar Silamé to attend *samaso*, the footrace among novices that is the festive highpoint during their seclusion in the lodge. Keba Dramé, my best informant and a prominent hunter and *marabout*, offered to accompany me to Misssera. The bicycle journey through forested flatland took all morning.

In Missera our host, Bakary Gitté, immediately dispatched his son Sajoba to escort me to the lodge, some two hundred yards from the village. I was overwhelmed by the ease of entering the enclosure, which in my thoughts had become such a forbidding place. Inside the deserted lodge and three days before leaving the field, I experienced true culture shock for the first time, perceiving something wholly alien either to my experience or expectation. The freshly severed head of an ox was propped against a wall next to the shank sections of the ox's legs. The odor had not yet become a stench but was strong and piercing. The bedding lined up on either side of the dirt floor was filthy and unkempt. Drums were scattered in one corner of the lodge. Smoke trailed upward from smoldering fires built in the open central corridor. The temperature in January could be relatively cool, sometimes dropping below 50° F, and the fires were needed to keep warm.

Sajoba took me quickly to the riverbank where the novices were about to plunge into the river, ritually washing themselves for the first time since their circumcision several days previously. The boys were startled when I appeared. One of them recognized me, calling out my name, and we exchanged greetings. This put the group at ease, since they had heard about me. The sight of the inch-wide circumcision wounds made me shudder with imagined pain. The white costumes, designed to protect the novice from cannibal-witches, were unlike anything I had ever seen. Within twenty-four hours I was able to see the footrace, the circumcision of one novice, and several other events that expanded my understanding of the total ritual.

I begin with this account to show how the process of fieldwork was for me an exceedingly gradual experience, with the most revealing observations of the society coming at the end of my stay. As they open themselves up to strangers, the Mandinko are not a particularly dramatic people. The lives of young men seem dominated by the drudgery of rudimentary farming, punctuated by prayer five times daily and by long hours of basket weaving during the winter months as harvesting is completed. Young women are occupied by cooking, washing clothes, caring for their babies, praying five times daily (although not in mosque) and the arduous physical labor of rice cultivation during the rainy season. As I acquired fluency in the language, the sense of drama in the society increased. The Mandinko are intensely religious and intellectual. Their rich language is perhaps best expressed in complex proverbs, riddles, historical legends, symbolically obscure circumcision songs, Islamic morality tales, and children's fables. Devout Muslims, they have none of the sculpture that is typical of more southerly forest peoples in West Africa. Yet their material culture is not unimportant to them. Their religious buildings have been carefully designed and maintained. The Mandinko also have a cult centered around the *kangkurao*. The *kangkurao* is the portrayal of a demon-figure by a mask-wearer who covers his body with the blood-red bark of the *fara* tree.[1] The figure, referred to conveniently as a mask, is accorded great power and is important in social control. I did not see a *kangkurao* mask until my second trip to Pakao and did not gain admission to this cult until after twelve months of fieldwork. I was considered a full member when the youths who make the mask allowed me to accompany them. During the first field trip, one informant finally agreed to show me how to make a *kangkurao* from *fara* bark only after we made a deal. The demonstration had to take place the day before I left the field. I promised not to reveal the informant's name and had to give him our two kerosene lanterns. Fearing that the village men might beat or kill him if they found out, my informant hid the bark in the forest after we stripped it, and brought it furtively to our hut late at night.

The Mandinko are outwardly friendly and hospitable to strangers, but are secretive about some of their ritual life and belief in evil spirits. In the early months, when insights came infrequently, my ability to do fieldwork was sustained by one idea: that somehow an understanding of Pakao society depended on a knowledge of which villages were most important to study. Through a stroke of luck, I was given the answer to this question from the very beginning.

Chris and I arrived in the provincial capital of Ziguinchor during July 1972, after a hot, all-day journey in a bush-taxi from Dakar and the customary delay crossing the Gambia River by ferry. We were given a place to stay by relatives of Bouly Dramé, a Senegalese Mandinko whom we had met a month earlier at the Conference on Manding Studies in London. We left open the question of precisely where to do fieldwork until our arrival, and wanted first to test the opinion of local informants. After two days of seeking advice unsuccessfully, we decided

---

[1] *Piliostigma thongii.* The *kangkurao* is discussed further in Chapter 5.

to take a trip across Mandinka territory to Sédhiou, once a colonial administrative
center and the area capital where Bouly Dramé had gone to primary school. It
was not an easy journey, involving overnight stays in Marsassoum and Sédhiou,
ferry trips across the Casamance and Songrougrou Rivers, and finally a return trip
across the Casamance by dug-out canoe. The villages around Marsassoum were
inhabited by both Jola and Mandinko people, and did not appear to be particularly
representative of any one ethnic group. In Sédhiou we learned of a village across
the Casamance named Karantaba, reputedly a famous Islamic center among Mandinko. On returning to Ziguinchor, we had practically decided to begin work
there. Yet Karantaba was not really a satisfactory choice either. It had a population
of over two thousand, and we preferred to start in a smaller village. We were also
concerned that Mandinka traditions might not be practiced in earnest in a place
where Islamic orthodoxy was taken so seriously.

We had a feeling of malaise and lack of direction that undermined morale at a
time when expectation was the only form of encouragement available. Hearing
that Bouly Dramé had unexpectedly returned to Ziguinchor from Dakar, we went
to see him and poured out our frustration, since it was on his advice that we had
first decided to study the Mandinko of Senegal. He was sitting in his compound
and listened patiently. We contended essentially that *we* ought to be returning to
America and that *he* ought to be doing Mandinka ethnography. He rejected this
plea, claiming that although he had been hoping to study his own people since
the 1940s, his life had become too complicated with two wives and seventeen
children, and he no longer had time. We raised the possibility of studying Karantaba, and he expressed serious concern. "This village is too serious to begin a study
without great difficulty," he said. "Even if I, native-born in Karantaba, were to go
with you, there are holy books and the tombs of holy men they would never show
you." He thought deeply for a moment and then spoke deliberately. "To understand
Pakao one has to live in three villages known locally as 'the triangle'—Dar Silamé,
Mankono Ba, and Soumboundou." We asked which village he would advise going
to first, and without hesitation he singled out Dar Silamé. He proposed that we
next live in Mankono and Soumboundou, and then in Karantaba only after we had
gained proficiency in the Mandinka language and were more experienced as field-
workers. I sensed that he knew much more than he was willing to tell. Deferring
completely to his greater knowledge, we decided to live in Dar Silamé first. "The
triangle" provided a strategy for our fieldwork and as a local concept it implied
to us a sense of centrality and geographic definition. "The triangle" became a sort
of code whose secret had to be unraveled. Its internal logic was always compelling,
even during periods of discouragement when other reasons for studying the Mandinko disappeared. We left for Dar Silamé the next morning.

The first trip to Dar Silamé had a sense of finality to it. There could be no easy
turning back. The bush-taxi let us off in Sakar and continued toward Kolda up
the one dirt road that bisects Pakao. In Sakar, a veteran of the French army—
there are a few in every Pakao village—greeted us in broken French. Serving as
a translator, he directed us to the Dar Silamé road, used infrequently by trucks
to carry off the peanut harvest, and he helped us to hire one man to carry additional baggage. It was well over 90° F during the five-mile walk to Dar Silamé

over a sandy road, and the weight of our backpacks forced us to rest several times. Even though it was noon, we had not imagined it would be so hot during the rainy season. We had expected the heavy cloud cover characteristic of July, but there were scarcely any clouds in sight. The forest looked unsatisfyingly thinned out, with few large trees. We had been told that the area around Dar Silamé was covered by plush jungle; instead, we found light scrub forest and an atmosphere pervaded by dryness. Chris and I talked about what Dar Silamé would look like. We steeled ourselves, thinking that perhaps our initial culture shock would be as severe as Chagnon's when he first met the Yanomamo.

The road broke out of the forest, passing open fields where people worked in the distance. The first building we saw was disappointing; it was a tin-roofed structure of European design, which in fact turned out to be a school. Otherwise, the village was obscured by a few enormous cotton trees, whose size presented a striking contrast with the saplings that predominate in the forest. A barefooted man dressed in rags, his work clothes, walked up and identified himself as *alkalo* (the chief), one of the few Mandinka words we had learned in Ziguinchor. He was an "assistant chief" who is often the genealogical son of a chief. The man led us to his father's house through some huts that had stone-like walls of mud-brick and thatch roofs. We were taken into the floor-level porch and presented to a remarkably old man, whom we presumed to be the chief. We sat and tried to look friendly, unable to speak a complete Mandinka sentence. The chief, named Fodé Ibrahima Dramé, spoke a few words to his son, looked at us deeply for a long while, and then broke the awkward silence by handing me a gourd full of milk. Surprised by the friendly gesture, I sipped lightly from the gourd, nervously feeling the hot, pungent milk run down my throat and assuming that I was well on my way to a good case of tuberculosis or undulant fever. The chief was wearing Muslim robes only somewhat less elegant than those I had seen in Dakar, and my first visual perceptions were not at all shocking. I had seen huts before; traditional housing is widespread in Senegal outside towns. During the several minutes we faced the chief, few words were spoken. It was after lunch, so the women had finished pounding grain with mortar and pestle. No, the first contact with this culture was much subtler than I expected, quiet and undramatic.

A student aged fourteen was summoned from a field to serve as a translator. He arrived as a small crowd was forming. An elder woman was surprised by Chris' long black hair and touched it. The chief asked that we all go into a near-by hut. We petitioned him for permission to live in his village for a few months, saying that Bouly Dramé had directed us there. The chief, whose own clan name was Dramé, pointed out with some pride that Bouly was his (classificatory) kinsman. As the chief spoke increasingly about Bouly, he became more sympathetic towards us. It was obvious that Bouly, a mid-level official in the Senegalese government, had achieved a fair amount of local fame. Wanting to demonstrate the personal importance of our relationship to Bouly, we decided to mention that he had given us the names Omar Dramé and Salimata Dramé. This pleased the chief and warmed the atmosphere further. The names stayed with us throughout our fieldwork, certainly making it easier for people to identify with us, for Dramé is easily the largest clan in Pakao and is the·chiefly family of both

Dar Silamé and Karantaba. The family name (*konton*) is always called out as a sort of punctuation between several formal greetings that grown Mandinko, regardless of age or sex, exchange when they meet. The Mandinka verb "to greet" is also *konton*.

The chief granted his permission and assigned us to the schoolmaster's quarters in the school, which were not used during the summer. He sent a gourd of rice for lunch, and several women and youths came to greet us, using the Dramé name and the required formal greetings. These were the first Mandinka phrases we learned. The first night in the school we heard a leopard snarling in the forest. Mice scampered across the floor, bats flew inside the house; our straw mattress was musty. It was indeed a long night!

I supposed every fieldworker must evolve a personal equilibrium between "going native" and complete detachment. During the first few weeks I found there were certain Mandinka notions I could not adjust to, such as eating with my hands and wearing a robe (pants were worn by only a few of the men my age). The first full day in Dar Silamé Chris and I thought that we might express our gratitude to the chief by working in his field. The Mandinka women were too aggressive in trying to recruit Chris to the rice fields about two miles from the village, and she thought it might be better if we both worked with the men in their peanut fields adjacent to the school. Neither of us fared very well. Mandinka men plough their fields by hand with steel-tipped hoes made by village smiths. The hoe handle is about three feet long, requiring the worker to bend over. After a couple hours of struggle in 90-degree weather, my back was in agony and my hands blistered. At lunchtime, bowls of water and millet broth were brought to the fields, and the men rinsed the mud off their hands. We took gourd spoons, squatted around the porridge, and quickly consumed the broth. Both of us hobbled back to bed thoroughly worn out. It took one more day of masochism before we brought this extreme of participatory observation to a halt. We were too exhausted to ask good questions and feared that our research would stagnate.

We were much more amenable to Mandinka housing than to farming. After two days, we realized that living at the school was unsatisfactory. Located just outside the village, it heightened our physical isolation during a period when observing was practically our only way to record facts. As we later learned, the school was held in suspicion by village elders, some of whom had opposed its construction seven years previously. Fortunately, a student named Boumba Cissé invited us to meet his parents and to live in a hut owned by them, solving the problem. Boumba's parents, Wandifa Cissé and Sanjiba Dramé, offered to share the household's meals with us. To our pleasant surprise, the hut was quite cool and had a fenced-in area behind it for washing, affording some privacy. This concept is not entirely Western, as is sometimes maintained; each house had such an area.

After setting up housekeeping, we looked for ways to increase our acceptance. Chris suggested that we plant a garden. This seemed to be a healthy adaptation to our desire to do some farming, and Mandinko themselves cultivate garden plots in the village. Our experience with the garden proved to us that failing is sometimes not a bad way to make friends. The first seedlings in the newly fenced-in plot attracted several visitors, including the village *imam* (mosque leader), who

Dar Silamé: At sunset, our host, Wandifa Cissé, drives his cattle from a watering hole to the pasture where they will spend the night.

asked us in marveling tones to describe the vegetables planted. Two well-known local disasters eventually befell the garden—goats and drought. To the delight of several elders, I was told one day in the central village square that goats had leaped the fence and eaten all the tomato plants. Drought killed the rest of the garden, and we harvested only a few very tough string beans. While it lasted, the garden was frequently a topic of conversation with our acquaintances, and when asked about it, we at least knew the Mandinka phrase, "There was too little rain and too many goats."

New experiences constantly entered my consciousness, and I was obliged to find some intellectually manageable way of thinking about them. Mandinko, for example, have a tendency to say "give me" something, such as sugar, money, or sandals, as a way of both teasing the owner and admiring the object. It was some time before I felt comfortable in giving an accepted polite reply, "There is not enough of it." As a way of greeting, the Mandinko ask, "Where are you going?" One should never elaborate, except to say either "home," "in the village," or "away from the village."

Sleep was a persistent problem. For more than a week we had no mattress in the Cissé hut, except for the traditional mat of woven bamboo that cut into our backs. We tried to soften it with newspapers, wooden plant presses, plastic rain-coats—all to no avail. I decided to travel to Ziguinchor in order to buy a foam rubber mattress. In the rainy season bush-taxis are infrequent, so I began the trip with a fifteen-mile walk in the hot midday sun. The mattress improved the situation, although not completely. Bats could be heard fluttering inside the house nearly every night I was in Pakao. On one occasion, the bat actually got inside the mosquito netting, which we tore down trying to get out. I never could completely adjust to the presence of bats. Keba Dramé once tried to explain away this uneasiness by saying that "to Mandinko a bat is as harmless as a chicken." Replying to Keba, I described the Westerner's feeling about bats by likening it to the more severe Mandinka fear of owls. The owl is synonymous in Mandinka culture with the hated cannibal-witch (*bwa*), a person who transforms into an animal shape for the purpose of consuming or molesting humans.

On the whole, our initial relationships with informants were not difficult ones, and these friends sometimes even volunteered information. Near the end of my first month in Dar Silamé, I was interviewing an elder named Arfan Sanji Cissé, while his visitor, Omar Sylla, listened with apparent interest. My genealogical questions prompted Omar to tell me about a book of Mandinko in Arabic script which outlined Pakao history.[2] This manuscript was in the possession of a relative in another Pakao village, and Omar offered to bring it to Dar Silamé. The manuscript, referred to locally as "the Pakao book," contained valuable historical information about the founders of early Pakao villages and their mosques, as well as nineteenth-century circumcision queens. Its pages contained prayers to Allah, and I later discovered that copies had been transmitted, probably by *marabouts*, to several other Pakao villages as if the manuscript were both a historical charter and a powerful religious charm. During the course of my fieldwork, the Pakao book came to represent (as well as anything) the devotion of the Mandinko to religion and to learning, to historical record keeping for its own sake.

The second example of an informant who offered his services demonstrates a different potential for the "first impression" and is ultimately tragic. Lamine befriended us during the first month of fieldwork. He was the only middle-aged man in the village who could communicate in workable French. He offered to serve as a translator and to show Chris medicinal plants in the forest. We had worked with him for about a week when Boumba Cissé confided to me that Lamine was "a little crazy" and that he was "now in a relatively calm period." This warning alarmed us, and we tactfully reduced our working relationship, although Lamine continued infrequent and brief visits for the purpose of formally greeting us. Unfortunately, within a month, it became obvious that Lamine was one of three village "madmen," and by far the most violent. He began to rave at other villagers in French and threatened them with his machete. He had a pathological hatred of black people and an irrational hero-worship for whites. He was said to have been disturbed since childhood, and Lamine himself attributed his misery to the early deaths of his parents and siblings. His racism was nurtured during several years of work for a French supervisor at the agricultural research station, SEFA. Ironically, he was sufficiently normal during this period, when he learned French, to have married. After his condition deteriorated, he left work and

---

[2] See Schaffer (1974).

Dar Silamé: Omar Sylla, great-grandson of the jihad *leader Syllaba, recites from his Koran in the village mosque.*

his wife divorced him, keeping their three daughters. During our time with Lamine, he erected poles in the central village square which he said were for the French to bring electric lights into the village. He set up a rod for an antenna and broadcast the news while pretending to read from a French magazine. He broke into the school and stole several Western items belonging to the schoolteachers, including a plastic canteen and French magazines, which he carried for weeks. When his rage reached unbearable intensity, he chopped off all the limbs of several enormous trees. Yet he never harmed anyone physically and never threatened us. He was beaten only once, by men who were angry because he had broken into the school. His antics were usually considered a form of entertainment, and he was shouted away only during the rare moment when his racist ravings became intolerable. During calm periods, villagers greeted him routinely.

More than any set of experiences, Lamine's case drove home to me that a fieldworker who enters a society not only becomes involved but has an effect, however incalculable that may be. I can only ponder the degree to which our entry into the village may have influenced the timing and severity of one of Lamine's relapses. The experience also forced me to appreciate how deceptive the first impression can be. The anthropologist is vulnerable and can be a victim of circumstances. The only response is to act humanly, to adapt, and to convert the experience into an insight. The capacity of Dar Silamé to tolerate Lamine and to deal with him humanely, even to appreciate him, is a lesson I shall not easily forget.

Our first field trip of five months produced some good data, thanks in large part to Chris' sensible approach to fieldwork. She painstakingly made a compass and pacing map of the village, revealing its structural design. Before going to the field, she made arrangements to have ethnobotanical specimens received at the Oxford herbarium, and saw to it that we received instruction in collecting and mounting plant material. From Chris' work in the field, it emerged that the Mandinko rely heavily on plant cures and have a sophisticated medical vocabulary. Chris also had the foresight to purchase a sturdy reel tape recorder. While she worked on the map and her ethnobotanical research, I concentrated on recording historical legends and conducted a genealogical survey of the village. We were able to help each other on these activities, and they had the added advantage of requiring simple skills in Mandinko.

Perhaps the greatest surprise to us during the initial fieldwork in Dar Silamé was the relative cooperation of informants and the considerable generosity of the family we lived with. We benefited from the Islam practiced in Pakao, where kindness to strangers is prescribed and *marabouts* consider both learning and travel for the sake of study to be virtues. There is a "host" system in Pakao, where travelers are customarily taken into a family and given food and lodging. A Mandinko who returns to another village always stays with the same host (*jatti*). The relationship between host and guest lasts a lifetime and may even be passed on to a succeeding generation.

On the first field trip, there were two persistent problems which simply could not be solved—drought and recording information on women. Our ability to learn about women was an index of our progress in learning Mandinko. During the early weeks, we were able to record some substantive information from the men

Dar Silamé: Shaded by mango trees, some women of Sylla and Cissé hamlets draw water from a well.

by working in French with male students as translators. This was obviously not feasible with the women, who did not speak French and who would never consent to talking about women's affairs with a young male translator.

The problem of drought is more difficult to describe. Rainfall had diminished during several years, reaching critical proportions in 1972 and precipitating the 1973 famine that focused world attention on the West African *sahel* region. Pakao lies in a forested zone within the southern fringe of this area. During our fieldwork, there was no outright starvation; the effects of the drought were more subtle. Food supplies were short, and there was great concern for crops. The rice crop almost totally failed, and villagers had little to eat besides millet and the seed from a locally cultivated grass. It did not rain during a two-week period in August, supposely the peak rainy month, prompting *marabouts* to read the Koran out loud for hours at mosque. With the onset of the dry season in November, restiveness increased as villagers struggled to deepen wells and to harvest their diminished crops. A riot nearly broke out when a wealthy cattle-owner slew an ox, as many villagers had not tasted meat for weeks. We were often hungry ourselves and could only barely supplement the basic diet with the few tins of tuna and sardines. It was probably fortunate that we left the field in December and did not return until early 1974.

On the return trip, I broadened my fieldwork as recommended by Bouly Dramé, living for about two months each in Mankono Ba, Soumboundou, and Karantaba. Many more acquaintances and working relationships were formed than can be described here, and I shall quickly summarize this phase before commenting on the final four months in Dar Silamé. In April Chris returned to England to continue her job making harpsichords in David Rubio's workshop near Oxford. She began cataloging plant specimens that I shipped from the field. Maps were drawn of the three villages, based on aerial photographs located in Dakar. In Mankono Ba and Soumboundou, I used a questionnaire to collect demographic data and attitudes about caste and class. In May, I was able to carry out my first substantive interviews with a female informant, Naba Sagnan, who talked with me about such subjects as circumcision, pregnancy, birth, child care, and accompanying medicines. Chris had worked with Naba on ethnobotany in March and April, and their friendship was the basis of Naba's willingness to cooperate with me. The spring and summer were spent investigating a host of subjects at the heart of our discipline, including marriage practices, kinship terms, inheritance, totemism, ethnomedicine, agricultural economics, politics, religion, witchcraft, and burial.

In October, the weather showed signs of turning cool, the rains had been plentiful, and the morale of villagers lifted as they waited for crops to mature. When I returned to Dar Silamé, it was with a sense of returning to home-ground. Other villagers in Pakao considered Dar Silamé to be my "host" village, and it was on the strength of relationships formed in 1972 that I began to learn details of the more secret subjects: slavery, *marabout* medicine, the *kangkurao* cult, and circumcision rituals. One subject, age-set organization, was not at all secret. But it is so complex that I was not able to understand it until after I did a quantitative study of the entire Dar Silamé system.

I felt the atmosphere of secrecy most keenly when interviewing Koto Fadera, for virtually everything she told me about women's affairs was a secret to be kept from men. I think her openness during weeks of daily interviews was due to her relative immunity from criticism. As circumcision queen, she had enormous power over the lives of women, a power not so much directly applied by commands as in being available to be consulted on any problem. This strength was enhanced by a commanding height of over six feet and by the great magical prowess that other villagers attributed to her. As a "wizard" (*kumfanunte*) Koto was able to perceive evil cannibal-witches and to slay them. She professed an ability to transform into a white cat in order to keep a protective eye on the women and girls of Dar Silamé. From the women's point of view, cannibal-witches can only be male, whether in human or animal form, so the men in Dar Silamé had a healthy respect for her ability to cause them bodily harm. Koto herself boasted, "The whole village is afraid of me, including the chief." In her hut she kept a magical staff that could kill cannibal-witches merely by touching them. She used this when watching over the female circumcision novices during their seclusion. The hunter Keba Dramé once approached the door of her house while I was interviewing, and seeing the magical staff, warily slipped away. Once I got over my own fear of working with Koto, her reputation tended to prevent anyone from challenging her cooperation with me.

One afternoon, the relationship with Koto broke down. Because of pressing work in the household, she refused to see me. I lost my temper and said she was "teasing, just fooling around with me." She refused to accept my apology that evening. I did not sleep that night, convinced that I had lost my most knowledge-able female informant. Rising early in the morning, I purchased some gifts, including relatively expensive peanut oil and boxes of refined sugar. I went to her hut with her son Nambaly, who pleaded that she accept the gifts as an assurance of my apology. Overnight she had fallen ill, and we found her still in bed with her mosquito netting pulled down. She answered fearfully and implied that I was a demon-spirit who had tried to injure her. Nambaly argued that the gifts were proof of good intention, and she finally relented. We resumed dis-cussions later as if nothing had happened.

It is not easy to escape the fieldworker's sustaining preoccupation "to learn more," and that means saturating oneself with interviews and, if necessary, the difficult negotiations that precede them. Yet one must somehow quietly turn off and slip into another frame of mind. Bicycle trips between villages offered one form of relief. The forest paths in Pakao are packed hard, and are well suited to this form of transportation. There are a few well-used bicycles in every village. Chris and I purchased bicycles at the beginning of the second field trip and traveled several hundred miles this way. Being alone in the forest, moving silently and quickly, gave an indescribable feeling of peace. Another distraction was to lie on one of several bamboo platforms in a village and unwind by focusing on the moon and the stars, which can be bright in the dry air. During most of my fieldwork in Pakao, I did this after supper for about a half hour.

Despite the need for respite, I gradually became more comfortable in Pakao. I had been to so many funerals and infant's naming ceremonies that technically there was no longer any need to attend them for the sake of recording new data. I nevertheless felt too isolated by staying away and rarely missed one. I developed a similar feeling about attendance at Friday mosque. I did not presume to have a sophisticated knowledge of Islam; adolescent males could write Arabic script and recite long passages of the Koran from memory. However, I felt serene going through the motions of saying prayers at mosque, even though I did not under-stand all the Arabic.

If there is one idea that appeals to an anthropologist doing fieldwork, it is the notion of a reliable informant who is also a friend. For me, the person closest to this description was Keba Dramé. Although considered a relatively young man of about forty, Keba was widely respected in the village as a hunter, *marabout*, plant healer, oracle, and wizard. His father Majima Dramé had been a famous Pakao chief in his day, and his name was synonymous with excellence as a hunter and *marabout*. Keba was Majima's youngest and favorite son, and the old chief had spent years teaching him. Keba was willing to spend days with me searching for medicinal plants or, in the privacy of his house, talking about any subject. As I grew to know him, it was obvious that he had perfected his reflexes, sensory perceptions, and sense of belief to an unusual extent. One reads about such persons in anthropological texts, but it was an unexpected experience in the field to witness such qualities and to hear other people attest to them.

Many informants claimed that Keba was unsurpassed at a dance called "the machete test." On the day of male circumcision in Dar Silamé, dancers stab them-selves with knives, but are protected from any injury by the strength of their belief and the magical charms they wear. In the performance of oracles I saw Keba astound his clients with prophecies. On one occasion during an interview, a dove perched on the roof of Keba's hut, and he spontaneously darted outside, listening intently to the bird's song. With absolute certainty he pronounced that a guest would arrive the next day. This indeed happened with the arrival of an old friend, a hunter named Lan Ndaye.

While I heard many tales of Keba's ability as a hunter, it still came as something of a shock to see him hunt. One morning in January 1975, Keba sent his friend Talibo Dramé to fetch me. I was told that Keba had killed a large antelope overnight and wanted to show it to me. Joining Keba and Lan Ndaye, we walked about two miles into the woods where Talibo spotted some wild turkeys which I could not see. Wanting to demonstrate his skill as a hunter, Keba ran silently into the brush and disappeared. After an interminable fifteen-minute wait, he fired his shotgun. He emerged from the brush with four wounded turkeys which he then killed with his knife. Keba explained matter-of-factly that he simply waited until four turkeys lined up in his sights. Lan Ndaye saw some more turkeys and tried to outdo Keba. Just before firing Lan made some noise, and I could hear the fluttering of wings as the birds scattered. He returned dejectedly with only one turkey. Keba casually cheered him up by claiming that he heard another one fall in a thicket about fifty yards away. Though none of us had heard the bird, Keba quickly found it.

Not far away, the "antelope" turned out to be a leopard. Keba had seen two leopards the previous night. Using the shotgun bequeathed to him by Majima, he wounded the male and trailed the female deep into the forest. Without finding her, he returned to the still dangerously thrashing male and slit its throat so as not to waste another shot. The carcass was left overnight. In the morning Keba removed the major bones and skinned the animal so that the sectioned meat could be repacked into the hide for convenient carrying. He excized the animal's bladder and forced urine out of it in the four directions. This was to leave a scent to attract other leopards to the spot, where he would be lying in wait.

Talibo Dramé had a theory about why Keba hunted leopards, and it says something about the Mandinka concept of a world torn by the threat of aggressive, evil magic (witchcraft, if you will) and the countering force of human action amplified and sustained by religious charms. Keba was nearly killed as a boy by a leopard, leaving a long scar deep in his forehead. Talibo explained that in fact the leopard was a cannibal-witch, an old woman who changed into the animal form for the express purpose of killing Keba. The old woman was slighted when the youthful hunter forgot a promise to provide her with meat. When the leopard attacked, Keba was so terrified that he threw down his gun. Left for dead, Keba was found in the forest and eventually healed by his father Majima. The chief then prepared a powerful charm of retaliation and with it slew the old woman. Talibo observed that Keba overcame his fear and now hunts leopards alone and at night. Talibo explained this transition as a result of one factor—charms. The charm, always prepared by a *marabout*, ultimately derives its strength from Allah, but seems also to have an independent power unto itself. Its capacity to defeat evil cannot exist purely at the level of belief and must be validated by

Dar Silamé: Keba Dramé has skinned his leopard, cut up the meat, and repacked it in the leopard's skin in order to carry it easily back to the village.

results; hence, Keba's success in hunting leopards. To illustrate the power of Keba's charms, Talibo seized on the most dramatic example he knew, the "shirt charm." This was a vest made of hand-woven cloth and covered by several individual charms. The shirt, later shown to me by Keba, was inherited through

Majima and was said to date from the late nineteenth century when it was used in battle. Drawing his explanation to a conclusion, Talibo asserted, "If Keba wears his shirt, a chain of men can hold on to him and not be injured." Talibo's description of the shirt illustrates the crucial link between Keba's uncanny success and the respect of his fellow villagers. Keba's struggles are not merely hunter against animal, but the conceptual embodiment of Mandinko against adversity in the world.

I would like to call Keba Dramé my friend, but such a description cannot adequately imply a fact about the field situation: relationships are built up by the anthropologist's desire to obtain information and skill in doing so, and by the informant's generosity in parting with what he or she knows. Rather, I finally ceased to think of Keba as an informant and began to consider him a person with whom I shared experiences. This sense is implied by the Mandinka word for friend, *kafotanyoma*, meaning "of the same group." I am not sure when we became *kafotanyoma*. Certainly this had happened by the time we rode bicycles to the circumcision ceremony at Missera and I had put away my notebooks, since there was no time to record things anyway. The return from Missera to Dar Silamé was not easy. After some six miles the path disappeared, and we were forced to ride through weeds more than seven feet tall, which had not been completely burned out by dry-season brushfires. It was getting dark, and Keba did not want to spend the night at the mercy of hyenas and leopards. He insisted he knew the way, and we pedaled as quickly as possible. The grass streaming between Keba's toes drew blood. We finally found the path to Dar Silamé just before nightfall. Exhausted and covered with scratches, blood, and soot, we collapsed on a bamboo platform where several men were sitting. One of them chuckled at the sight of dirt smudged on my face (soot is, of course, nearly invisible on Mandinko). With mirth in his voice, he remarked, "You sure are a white man," as if the realization suddenly dawned on him in a way he had not thought of before.

The next day, as I prepared to leave the field, a problem developed. Chief Fodé Ibrahima Dramé was unhappy with my decision to give a bicycle each to Keba Dramé and to my host Wandifa Cissé. Recalling the hours he had spent recounting oral traditions, he argued, "According to our Mandinka way of learning, your best gifts should go to your teacher and your host. Keba is merely your *kafotanyoma*." I offered the chief my foam rubber mattress, and explained to him that Keba had never asked for compensation.

The next morning I said good-bye to the several people who had helped me. Koto Fadera, who died of tuberculosis within a month, was lying in bed, coughing up phlegm and breathing with great difficulty. The chief said he was peaceful about my decision on the three major gifts. Struggling to be philosophical, he declared, "All of the people in this village are my younger siblings, my children and my grandchildren. Whatever you give to them is a gift to me." Keba Dramé and his *kafotanyoma* Talibo Dramé walked me out of the village to a spot where the dirt road rose and began curving out of sight. As is the custom in Pakao, we extended hands outward, palms up, spit lightly into them, rubbed our faces, and uttered a last prayer.

2/Pakao: The setting

THE TRIANGLE

I have said that the location of my fieldwork was determined by an indigenous notion of three villages which are known locally as "the triangle." In Pakao thought, this triangular concept implies centrality and makes geography the embodiment of religious symbolism. The three villages which comprise "the triangle," Dar Silamé, Mankono Ba, and Soumboundou, do in fact form a triangle near the geographic center of Pakao. Jeta Camera, the chief of Soumboundou, explained that the three villages epitomize the whole of Pakao. "When you hear the word Pakao," he said, "you think of these three villages." Informants described the centrality of the villages in several ways. They were called the "navel" of Pakao and "the head of the liver." Another commonly used phrase symbolically identifies the villages as "the three stones of the cooking fire," which in women's cook-houses are always laid in the shape of a triangle.

The local explanation for the fact that the villages are important is essentially religious. Informants stress that Allah answers the prayers offered in the three villages, whose mosques are believed to have special powers. This explanation by a slave caste man in Dar Silamé is characteristic: "Allah answers the prayers of these three villages. A prayer to Allah offered in the three mosques will be answered if one is patient. You may also curse the man who harms you with your own prayer."[1] Fodé Ibrahima Dramé, the chief of Dar Silamé, relied on a different, almost mythological image to describe the religious importance of the three Pakao villages. He said that "according to the ancestors there is an opening into heaven, and these three villages frame its entrance."

It is conceivable that the religious symbolism of "the triangle" derives from the historical prominence of the villages. Arfanba Sagnan of Mankono Ba seemed to imply this when he said that "Allah has favored us over neighboring villages." He added that in the nineteenth century the villages formed a common defense against raiding and pillaging. I was often tempted to look for sociological or historical explanations of the triangle. For example, Dar Silamé played the leading role in the 1843 *jihad*, and also traces its ancestry to Karantaba. Mankono Ba traces descent from Keita, the royal clan of the Mali Empire. Soumboundou also traces

---

[1] The Pakao word for "prayer" may also mean "curse" and has a profound importance in the society. See *dua* in the section below on local Islam.

descent directly from Mali and is well-known locally as a village dominated by artisans and praise-singers. Such interpretations, however, were my own and were never offered by any informants. In Pakao thought "the triangle" is ultimately a theological concept.

RIVER AND TERRAIN

The southern border of Pakao is marked by the Casamance River. The river's name is from the Mandinko, meaning "King of Cassas" and refers to the kingdom of Cassas encountered in the fifteenth and sixteenth centuries by Portuguese explorers. The kingdom still existed in the 1840s, although in diminished size (Bertrand-Bocandé 1849:336). Except for a word list and some historical comments by Bertrand-Bocandé, almost nothing has been recorded of the Cassas people.

The Casamance River is about 160 miles long from its mouth on the Atlantic to its source east of Kolda. It is at least one-half mile wide all the way to Soumboundou, some 100 miles upriver. Above Sédhiou the river is shallow in places; it was thus impossible in colonial times for large sailing vessels to navigate into Pakao.

Fish from the Casamance River are a vital source of protein for the Mandinko. Fish are consumed along with rice or some other grain practically every day and in 1974 could be purchased inexpensively for about six cents (15 CFA) per kilo.

Mankono Ba: Forming a large circle in the shallow waters of the upper Casamance, the men drive the fish to the center. Then, as shown in the photograph, they simultaneously lift their hand-held nets and later string the fish on cords attached to the waist.

*Soumboundou: Two youths fish in the Casamance River from their dugout canoe.
The weighted, circular net can be quickly drawn back to the boat and cast again.*

The most effective means of fishing involves a group of ten to twenty men, who wade in the river toward the center of a circle where they scoop up the fish in hand-nets. The men also fish with a weighted circular net tossed from a canoe or by casting a barbed spear into reeds along the riverbank.

The river is not the object of any reverence or important myth and is viewed mainly as an obstacle to be crossed. The heavy dug-out canoes are used for fishing and for crossing the river, but not for traveling up- or downstream.

In former times the river provided freshwater irrigation to an elaborate system of rice paddies. The remnants of this system are quite striking around Soumboundou, where the dikes are still used as paths through the shallow water near the river's edge. Since the 1960s, successive years of drought are said to have caused the river to become too saline, making it useless for irrigation. The diminished rainfall in recent years has increased the tidal nature of the river. During the dry season, so little water flows into the river that it has virtually no downstream current. Informants say that prior to the drought rice could be grown along the river for ten months out of the year. The Pakao Mandinko now cultivate rice in land-locked paddies dependent on the summer rainy season for water. Rice can be cultivated all year round only near two villages where springs are located.

The land of Pakao is fairly level, with gradual hills and low areas. The highest point in Pakao (some bluffs near Soumboundou) is no more than seventy-five feet above the river. The soil is rich in clay, and there are pockets of limestone. Clay is used to make pots, and the limestone is used in plastering houses. The naturally hard topsoil is also used for building the walls of houses. During the dry-season months of March and April, soil is made into brick merely by mixing it with water and pouring it into a wooden mold. These bricks are laid with mortar made from the same mud. The houses are built in round or square designs and roofed with thatch.

The land between villages is covered by light forest. There is not much undergrowth due to brush-fires set by hunters during the dry season to eliminate hiding places for game. The forest around villages has been cleared for up to a mile to permit cultivation.

POPULATION SIZE AND ADMINISTRATION

There are difficulties in determining the population of a Pakao village. Villages tend to be large, averaging about a thousand people each. Even local inhabitants have trouble distinguishing between temporary travelers and permanent immigrants. The Mandinko are prone to making extended journeys lasting from a few days to several years. Mandinka women on occasion raise their children in villages of their kinfolk before rejoining their husbands. The men travel seeking work, or for the purposes of study or making a religious pilgrimage. In a survey of the population of Dar Silamé in 1972, I counted 1001 persons. This figure includes several people who were traveling temporarily at some time during the survey. For the same year, the local administration recorded a much lower population figure of 508.[2] There is a simple explanation for the discrepancy. The census, conducted biannually, is used for collecting tax. A head tax of about two dollars and forty cents (600 CFA) must be paid annually by every man, woman, and adolescent, causing the men to conceal additional marriages and newly born children who will eventually become part of their tax liability. People older than about seventy-five and younger than ten are exempt from the tax. Students and the disabled are also exempt. Villagers do not report some of the exempt persons to census-takers, "since they are not taxed anyway."

The smallest Pakao villages, Bani and Ida, have about 200–250 persons. Diana Ba (Jena Ba), the largest village, has roughly 3500 people. It is possible for a Pakao village of less than 200 people to thrive for a time. In 1974, a year after it was founded, Taiba had a population of forty-three. In 1969, the year before it disbanded, the village of Kounkali had a population of twenty-three, according to figures provided by the local administration at Djendé. The last four heads of families in Kounkali included a chief, an *imam*, and a smith. In addition to being farmers, these men appear to represent the minimum occupational diversity needed to constitute the male contingent of a village. Drought, as well as relative isolation from the one road bisecting the country, probably facilitated Kounkali's decline.

The earliest population estimates for villages in the Pakao vicinity are recorded

---

[2] This figure was provided by the Djendé *arrondissement*.

by Hecquard in 1850 (1855:90, 128, 129, 134). He estimated that the largest villages had about 2000 inhabitants and it can be inferred that the smallest had somewhere between 200 and 500. The population extremes of today are not that much greater than they were in 1850. It is conceivable that the current average population of about 1000 was characteristic of villages in 1850.

The estimated population now living in the area of the former Pakao kingdom is about 20,000. A majority of these people trace their ancestry to Mandinka stock, and all of them speak Mandinko. There are still some significant examples of non-Mandinka lineages that have been assimilated. The Dramé, the most populous single lineage in Pakao, are of Sarahollé origin. The Baro and Soli are of Fula origin, while the Sylla are of Jakhanké extraction. It is also said that "many people have some blood of the Bainuk." These original inhabitants of the region were reputedly assimilated or else driven out during the *jihad*.

Pakao is bordered on the east by the Fula people, whose territory is called Fuladu, or Feridu after the former kingdom. Elsewhere, Pakao is entirely surrounded by Mandinko who live in villages on the south bank of the Casamance in Balma-dou and Suna, and in adjacent villages in Boudié, Jasine, Jasori, and Sungkodu. All of these areas were non-Muslim kingdoms until such political systems were destroyed during the *jihads* of the nineteenth century. Villagers in the six former kingdoms bordering Pakao still refer to their area by the name of the kingdom. The six bordering kingdoms are also said to lie in the territory of Pakao. A map drawn in the 1840s (Bertrand-Bocandé 1849) suggests that the extension of the name Pakao to adjacent territory happened after the *jihad* of 1843. This was possibly because of the prestige associated with the original Pakao kingdom where the *jihad* was started. Muslims in the adjacent areas may also have wanted to dissociate themselves from the non-Muslims who formerly ruled them.

Administratively, Pakao lies in the department of Sédhiou, named for its capital. The department is divided into five districts. The one administered from Djendé, near Sédhiou, subsumes Pakao. Karantaba, lying in Suna on the south bank, is in the Tanaff district. The head of a district supervises the census and tax, provides identity cards, and in some instances resolves disputes.

Pakao is bisected by the Sédhiou to Kolda road, which is unpaved as far as Diana Malari and runs about a mile north of the river. Bush-taxis make the trip between Sédhiou and Kolda almost daily. Sédhiou, Kolda, and Diana Malari have markets that are regularly visited by Pakao villagers. Each has telecommunication services and an infirmary. The department of Sédhiou lies in the broader admin-istrative scope of Casamance, one of seven Senegalese provinces. The capital of Casamance is Ziguinchor, a town occasionally visited by Pakao villagers to obtain consumer goods, medical attention, or ammunition. A paved road called the trans-Gambian highway connects Ziguinchor with the national capital, Dakar. Both the Casamance and Gambian Rivers must be crossed by ferry. Dirt roads link Sédhiou and Pakao to the paved system.

Since the 1960s all but a few Pakao villages have had two full-time teachers and two concrete-block school buildings for two levels of elementary pupils. Nearly all of these students are male. Girls are permitted by law to attend the school system, but in general they are not allowed to do so by the male and female leadership of the village.

SUBSISTENCE

Pakao is primarily a sedentary, agricultural society dependent on a good rainy season for a successful harvest. The line between a good and bad season is a fine one. In 1972, considered a disastrous year, it rained a total of 785 mm. During the "plentiful" years of 1973 and 1974 it rained 983mm and 894mm respectively.[3] While the quantity of rain is important, the duration of the season and regularity of rain is equally important. In 1972 the rains were erratic. Normally the rainy season begins in the first week of June, is heaviest in July and August, and diminishes to negligible quantities by October.

There are five staple crops: rice, millet, peanuts, corn, and *digitaria*,[4] a domesticated native grass. Rice, cultivated exclusively by women, is the favorite Mandinka food. In June and early July the women prepare a rice field by turning the soil with a long-handled hoe. Planting follows immediately. In August and September the women transplant the rice shoots to less water-logged fields. Harvesting begins in September and is continued through October. The rice without its hull (white rice) is cooked by steaming and boiling and is flavored with a number of sauces, most often the favored peanut gravy. A white dough called *munko* is produced from rice flour, and is distributed among males at ceremonial gatherings.

The men cultivate peanuts and millet. The two crops are planted either in alternate rows or separate fields. In June and July the men plough their fields with a short-handled hoe. The first weeding takes place in August, and the second occurs later in September. Harvesting begins in October. Ironically, a heavy rainy season washes away organic materials in the soil, making it hard and difficult to work. Peanut plants can be removed only by ploughing them out by hand, prolonging the completion of the harvest until December, as was the case in 1974.

The uprooted peanut plants are left in place to dry for a few days. Then the farmer carries his plants with a long stake to a central area in the field and places them in a circular pile to dry further. This pile is enclosed in a bamboo fence to keep out both wild and domestic animals. The plants are then threshed with two sticks to knock off the peanuts. The farmer separates the peanuts from the remaining chaff by winnowing them in a strong breeze. The peanuts are bagged in the field and transported into the village, where they are weighed for sale.

Millet is the most durable crop in times of famine, when it is consumed as a broth for all three meals. It is otherwise the predominant Mandinka breakfast food. Millet is easy to harvest. In order to cut off the millet ear, the farmer simply knocks down the entire millet stalk. The women prepare the millet by pounding it with mortar and pestle and threshing it in a shallow bamboo basket. Rice is prepared in similar fashion. However, the women thresh *digitaria* with their feet on the porch area of a house. Both the millet and *digitaria* are cooked by boiling. The millet broth is flavored with milk or rich cream and with a variety of gathered fruits. The *digitaria* is topped with peanut gravy or a sauce made of wild herbs. Corn is the most important crop planted in village gardens. These small, bamboo-

---

[3] The figures were provided by officials of the Karantaba rice cooperative.
[4] In Mandinko, *findo (Digitaria exilis)*.

Karantaba: Using a small hoe, a farmer plants his peanut crop the morning after the first hard rain of the season.

Dar Silamé: Two farmers winnow the chaff from the peanuts in a brisk wind.

fenced gardens lie in proximity to the households of more senior heads of families. The corn is ripe in September, early enough for a second crop of tomatoes to be planted in its place. The tomatoes are used for sauces; the corn is eaten roasted or is pounded into a meal and consumed as a broth or as couscous.

The fields and gardens are left to fallow for relatively short periods, ranging from one to five years. This timing depends on the judgment of the farmer, who knows that land left to fallow too long will be difficult to clear. On occasion the farmer plants a field for two consecutive years. Villagers are able to improve yields of peanuts by using natural and some artificial fertilizer. New fields are regularly slashed and burned at the perimeter of land under cultivation. The Mandinko have a clever system for storing the harvest. They place grains to be eaten in the near future in the granary area on the second floor of the women's cook-house. To store grain for several months, villagers place it in large baskets sealed with a mixture of cow dung and ashes.

Farming is an honored occupation in Mandinka society. Everyone except the infirm tills the soil. The Mandinko tell legends about those few men and women who regularly achieved extraordinary harvests. Strength and luck, two virtues in Mandinka society, are attributed to the successful farmer. The Mandinko also take great care to avoid waste. One of the principal jobs of the younger boys is to serve as look-out from towers in peanut and millet fields. It is their duty to chase off marauding wild pigs and monkeys. The older boys scrupulously keep the cattle away from crops. During the rainy season cattle are not even allowed near water holes, where they might trample maturing crops. Instead, the Mandinko laboriously water their cattle in a designated pasture by manually carrying heavy buckets for distances of a half-mile or more.

Peanut farming is uniquely important to Mandinka society since it is the prin-

Dar Silamé: A girl in Sylla hamlet rolls peanut butter, which the Mandinko boil into a delicious sauce. The large notched log behind the girl is a ladder to the granary on the upper level of her cook-house.

cipal source of cash (CFA) in the village economy. The CFA is the monetary unit of Senegal and most of France's other former colonies in West Africa, and it is tied to the franc at a rate of 50:1. There are about 250 CFA to the dollar. Since the 1960s, most Pakao villages have had a cooperative association which organizes the sorting and weighing of each farmer's peanuts. Between December and March a local representative of ONCAD, the government farming organization, buys the harvest at a fixed price per kilo. If the government resale of the crop can be negotiated for a higher price on the world market, a rebate of 1–5 CFA per kilo is paid out to farmers by the purchasing agent in the summer. From 1970 to 1974 the purchase price per kilo was 17 CFA, 17 CFA, 22 CFA, 28 CFA, and 40 CFA for each year, respectively. In 1970 and 1971 there were rebates of 1 and 3 CFA. To examine the records for one year, in 1972 Dar Silamé farmers harvested 210,756 kilos of peanuts, excluding those reserved for personal consumption. The ONCAD headquarters in Sédhiou received 9,208 kilos as reimbursement for fertilizer provided to the village cooperative. The cooperative sold 201,548 kilos to ONCAD at a price of 22 CFA per kilo, bringing 4,434,056 CFA into the village, about $17,736.[5] Since 1972 some corn, oranges, and mangoes have also been sold to private companies, earning as much as 100,000 CFA for a village in a given year.

What do villagers buy with the money they earn from the peanut crop? The most popular local consumer good is refined sugar. This is used almost exclusively to flavor millet broth. Kola nuts, salt, cooking oil, tobacco, cigarettes, biscuits, and kerosene are also sold by the village merchant. The relatively well-off villager might travel to Sédhiou to buy metal bowls, buckets, tin roofing, or a bicycle.

To supplement their staples, the Mandinko have many foods available on a seasonal basis. These include okra, red peppers, tomatoes, and other vegetables grown in village gardens and a variety of plants gathered from the forest. Mandinko slaughter their livestock sparingly as if there were some religious or special significance to them, while in fact, probably because of Islam, there is none. Chicken, goat, and sheep are eaten mostly during rituals, religious festivals, and work feasts. An ox is slain only during male circumcision or the funeral of an important elder. Cattle are an important symbol of wealth and are preserved for their prestige and capital value. The milk they provide is consumed in rather small quantities and is often curdled for use in millet broth. The total size of the Dar Silamé herd in 1972 was a substantial 236 head.[6] The tendency to preserve cattle means that people eat much less meat than they would like. The three or four hunters per village meet only a fraction of the demand by killing deer, antelope, and occasionally a leopard. Chicken is eaten no more than once every two weeks; sheep and goat are eaten perhaps once a month; and beef is rarely available to an individual more than once a year. In short, grains and vegetables are the substantial part of the diet.

TIME

The Mandinko mix both Muslim and non-Muslim ideas in naming the seasons, months, days, and times of the day. To sort out Muslim influences, one must rely on a combination of sources, interpretations by informants, and the presence of Arabic words.

[5] The figures were provided by ONCAD, Sédhiou.
[6] This figure was provided by the livestock division of the Agriculture Department in Sédhiou. The census is taken during an annual vaccination.

The calendar is lunar, and there are four seasons with three lunar months each. The four seasons are "the harvest," "the dry season," "the rainy season," and "the dusty season." There are two principal seasons, "the dry season," subsuming "the harvest"; and "the rainy season," which includes "the dusty season." Mandinko count years in terms of rainy seasons. In Mandinka calculations of time the most obvious evidence of an Islamic idea is an Arabic word. The words for the seasons are Mandinko rather than Arabic, suggesting a system of non-Muslim origin. This seems to be equally true of the naming system for the months of the year. I could find Islamic interpretations for the names of only two of the months, "praise the prophet" and "the fasting month." Curiously, the same informant gave "youthful moon" as a second, possibly non-Muslim meaning for the latter month. No obvious single idiom pervades all the names of the months, although some of them are images of growth and maturation.

Informants ordered the months according to two different systems, the one beginning with "the moon of drink" and the other with "the elder woman." The first is a Muslim way of ordering the months in which the year begins at the conclusion of the month of Ramadan (see Delafosse 1929:287). This month often occurs during autumn. Delafosse concluded that the months are also ordered in a non-Muslim fashion, beginning "with the appearance of the first moon to follow winter solstice, or about January 1st" (1929:286). Thus, in Pakao many informants listed the months of the year beginning with "the elder woman." The progression of the seasons does make more ecological sense if one begins at the non-Muslim starting point, proceeding from "dry" to "wet" to "dusty" and concluding with the "harvest."

The names of the seven days of the week are Arabic language imports. They are *alhado* (Sunday), *tenengo* (Monday), *talato* (Tuesday), *arabo* (Wednesday), *aramiso* (Thursday), *arajimo* (Friday), and *sibito* (Saturday). The holiest day is Friday, when mosque is attended by all able-bodied males. Thursday is a holy day

TABLE 1   SEASONS AND MONTHS OF THE YEAR

I. *tilikando* The dry season	A. *sanjano* The harvest	1. *minkaro*, the moon of drink 2. *banakono*, pregnant, (nearly) rich 3. *bana*, the wealthy man
	B. *tilikando* The dry season	4. *musakoto*, the elder woman 5. *kekoto*, the elder man 6. *anabisoko*, Praise the prophet
II. *sama* The rainy season	C. *sama* The rainy season	7. *anola*, the successor 8. *anola fulanjao*, the second successor 9. *arajebekono*, Araje is pregnant
	D. *kunchamaro* The dusty season	10. *arajabo*, Araje gives birth 11. *sunkary kono*, the pregnant girl's month, or before *sunkaro* 12. *sunkaro*, youthful moon, or the fasting month

also, and ceremonial white rice bread is distributed in the evening. Koranic school is held on Friday and on each successive day through Tuesday.

The various times of the day mix both Muslim and non-Muslim ideas. The most obvious Islamic imports are the names for the five daily prayers: *suba* (5 a.m.), *selfana* (2 p.m.), *alansaro* (5 p.m.), *fitero* (7 p.m.), and *safo* (8 p.m.). The especially devout Muslims say a sixth prayer, called *wuliha*, at about 10 a.m. The non-Muslim portion of the daily nomenclature refers to natural events, such as "the first crowing of the cock" (2 a.m.), "first light" (4.30 a.m.), "sunrise" (5.30 a.m.), "noon" (1 p.m.), "sunset" (6.30 p.m.), and "the beginning of night" (7.30 p.m.). Unlike our reckoning of a day, beginning at midnight, the Pakao day is variously reported to begin between "the first crowing of the cock" and "daybreak." Babies born in the very early morning in Western time are considered by Mandinko to have been born on the previous day.

THE *MARABOUT*

In Mandinka society the *marabout* is an Islamic cleric who plays a major role as a healer and as a religious counselor. The Mandinka word for this person is *moro*. The term *marabout* is more widely used in French speaking West Africa and is also understood by Mandinko themselves. The *marabout* is often possessed of supernatural qualities. He is a wizard and is thus able to foretell the future, to interpret natural signs, and to identify cannibal-witches masquerading in human or animal form. Often he is an expert in plant medicine. The *marabout* can provide formal counsel by recounting a morality tale known through oral tradition or by reading from a hand-written, usually inherited "book of advice." The *marabout* is always a teacher, instructing his own sons or a larger group of pupils in the literal and interpretive meanings of the Koran.

Considering their sharpened sense of perception, it is perhaps logical that many *marabouts* are oracles. The Mandinka word for oracle, *jubero*, literally means "seeing." Mandinka oracles foretell the future by interpreting the patterns of seven red, elongated beans dropped on the ground or by reading the pattern formed by four notched sticks thrown in a gourd of water. The sticks represent "boy," "girl," "elder man," and "elder woman." I once heard Keba Dramé tell a hunter during a stick oracle that his wife was pregnant; this astonished the hunter, who believed the information was still a secret. Keba also foretold that the hunter would suffer a serious illness and would recover only if he delivered portions of the antelope he killed to his village elders as alms. Some *marabouts*, such as Keba and his father Majima, are also hunters. Their skill in the forest is said to be linked to their sensory powers as wizards.

In addition to his counseling role, the *marabout* is able to prevent and to cure illness or injury inflicted by mortals or by evil spirits. He does this by preparing four types of charms. The most widely used is the "written charm." A collection of these charms is contained in a copybook passed on from *marabout* to son. The *marabout* duplicates the written charm from a master copy, which includes the medicinal message in Arabic script and also directions for where the charm should

Mankono Ba: The hunter Baba Sagnan, a marabout *and trusted informant, leaves a village path on his way to the forest.*

be worn on the body or placed in the environment. Not surprisingly, the leather-covered charms are believed dangerous if used by an enemy, requiring a Mandinko to wear anticharm charms. This sort of charm is called "body guardian," suggesting self-defense. Keba Dramé said that two of his most commonly purchased charms specifically caused death or the burning of a village. Additional written charms from the warfare era, still found in contemporary copybooks, are designed to con-

Karantaba: Lan Soli Bantanjao, a skilled hunter, marabout, *and medicinal expert, uncovers the root of the* bilungkujiba (Marinda geminata rubia), *used in making blue dye. His rifle is a muzzle-loading flintlock, not an uncommon weapon in Pakao.*

vert pagans or to protect the wearer from bullets if properly sewn into the flesh of his leg. Keba said that his father wore this leg charm.

The key feature of a second type of charm is water. A water charm is duplicated from the master copy onto a writing board, and the wet ink is then washed into a bowl. The client drinks the solution or rinses it over his body. The Mandinka penchant for washing and bathing probably accounts for the popularity of this charm. Most, but not all, written charms can also be used as "water charms."

A third sort of charm is a string blessed by a *marabout* and worn on the body. It was said that a string charm could be assigned any purpose; however, I saw it used in mainly two instances. In the first, the blessed string was placed on the wrist of an infant hours after birth to protect it from evil spirits. Secondly, string charms were placed on the tails of cattle after several deaths in the herd raised fears of an epidemic, again caused by evil spirits. Many people in Dar Silamé feared for themselves during this time and also wore the string charms.

The last sort of medicinal charm is the personal blessing of a *marabout*. Such a blessing "can turn any object into a medicine" or can be applied directly without an accompanying object. To bless someone, the *marabout* spits lightly on the forehead of the patient and presses it with the palm of a hand, often the right hand.

The widespread use of charms is one indication of the great danger that Mandinko perceive in their world. Much of the danger is due to demon-spirits (*gino*), which can bring death and suffering to humans. "Everything, every person has a demon-spirit." People are shadowed by these spirits, and one of the principal duties of the *marabout* is to protect his clients from them with various charms and blessings. This is not easy. Whole villages such as Karantaba, Soumboundou, and Dar Silamé have double villages of demon-spirits lying nearby. In Pakao the especially religious places have more, not fewer, demon-spirits; the presence of demon-spirits validates the ability of *marabouts* to control them. Karantaba, the holiest Pakao village, has a reputation for having the most dangerous demon-spirits. Its mosque is thought to shelter many demon-spirits at night and is the only Pakao mosque off-limits after dark. The fifth, night-time prayer cannot be said there. On one occasion I witnessed, a tornado believed to be a demon-spirit swept perilously close to the Karantaba mosque just as the men rose to say Friday prayers. Two houses were demolished. A frightened Wolof pilgrim told me later, "This village is too dangerous: it is the holiest village in Senegal."

LOCAL ISLAM

Most Mandinka religious words are Arabic in origin, but Islam as practiced locally also contains variations of Muslim orthodoxy. Students of Arabic will recognize the derivation of the Mandinka words for "heaven" and "hell," *arajena* and *jahanama*, from the Arabic *janna* and *jahannam*. The Mandinko for "prayer," *salo*, is from *salah*; "alms," *sada*, is from *sadaqa*; "cemetery," *kaburo*, is from *kabr* the Arabic for "grave." Other etymologies are more dubious: is the Mandinko for "soul," *nio*, from *niyyah*, the Arabic for "intention"? Is the Mandinko for "fasting," *sungo*, from the Arabic *sawm*? At least one major religious concept

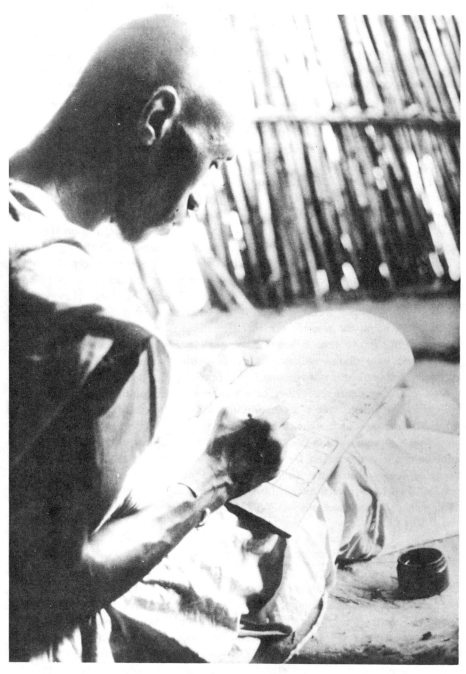

Dar Silamé: Keba Dramé prepares a water charm by writing his potion on a wooden tablet and then rinsing it into a bowl.

among the Mandinko seems to have no real parallel in Arabic, nor in Islam. This is the concept of purgatory, *singa*, a region of the afterlife between heaven and hell.

The most direct and renewable link with orthodox Islamic ideology is the pilgrimage to Mecca. Several Pakao villages have two or three *marabouts* who have made this journey. Two of the more famous were El Hadj Fodé Alemamé Dramé and El Hadj Kaoussou Soli who traveled from Karantaba by freighter to Mecca and stayed there ten and twenty-eight years respectively. Both men speak Arabic fluently. Four Islamic festivals are observed each year. The most important of these is the month of Ramadan, celebrated throughout the Muslim world and marked by ritual fasting. Another festival is Tabaski, often occurring in December or January and highlighted by the ritual slaying of rams. The Mandinko in Pakao also celebrate the prophet's birthday in the spring by parading with a banner from the mosque to the *imam*'s house. Another festival occurs in February or March and is marked by public reading of the Koran and the exchange of gifts among cross-cousins. There is an interesting local adaptation of Islam during Tabaski day and on the final day of Ramadan. The males and elder women of Pakao villages proceed solemnly in single file to a sacred tree or group of trees east of their villages in order to say the traditional Muslim prayers. These trees, used as prayer-sites for decades, are believed to shelter protective demon-spirits.

In Pakao there are two types of religious buildings, a mosque and a prayer house. According to legend, the smaller prayer house was the first religious structure built in a village and was usually replaced by a mosque. However, for particular reasons two Pakao villages have a prayer house in addition to a mosque. In Dar Silamé the prayer house covers the grave of Syllaba, the *jihad* leader. A larger prayer house in Karantaba houses the grave of Fodé Heraba Dramé, the founder of the village and of its first Pakao mosque. Pilgrims visit both sites and remove small quantities of earth from the tombs for medicinal purposes.

Prayer houses tend not to be more than about fifteen feet square, although the one recently constructed in Karantaba to replace the previous structure is larger. The Pakao mosque is the largest structure in a village, where it is imposing compared with the size of an ordinary dwelling. Pakao mosques are said to have been built in the nineteenth century, prior to the lifetimes of individuals living today, and several of the mosques are larger than twenty square feet. The mosque is built of mud bricks and is plastered white. These buildings normally have a covered porch on at least one side. In several of the mosques a brick staircase has been built to the ceiling. Prior to the 1960s the stairs led to a hole in the thatched mosque roof, permitting the crier to call prayers from a high place. In recent years most Pakao mosques have been roofed in corrugated iron, and the crier now stands at the bottom of the stairs. Worshipers line up on the porch areas and between the rows of pillars inside the mosque. All Pakao mosques are surrounded by palisade fences. No one mentioned any special significance to the fences, except that "they keep out the chickens and goats." I thought they resembled the stockades around Pakao villages described by nineteenth-century observers during the warfare era. No informant, however, could confirm my suggestion that perhaps the fences represented militant Islam.

Pakao is well-known in Senegal for its mosques and prayer houses, and as I have mentioned in the Introduction Pakao Muslims consider their land holy. They justify this belief with basically two religious ideas: "The *dua* of Pakao are great." "In this land *dua* are answered." The Pakao word *dua*, meaning roughly "prayer of intercession," is from the Arabic *du a*. Wehr defines this Arabic word in the following terms: "invocation of God, supplication, prayer; request, plea; good wish; imprecation, curse" (1971:283). The Pakao word has much the same meaning, and the *dua* is highly regarded as a powerful force. *Dua* are said to have killed one Dar Silamé schoolteacher and critically injured another in a highway accident. Considered lazy, the teachers were blamed during public meetings for the poor performance of their students. Speaking of the accident, one elder confided to me, "When you are on bad terms with Dar Silamé, its *dua* will kill you."

The affirmative value of *dua* is believed just as strongly regardless of social position. One man of slave caste from Dar Silamé stressed the importance of the Pakao triangle villages by invoking the idea of *dua*: "Their *dua* are the most powerful. When their *dua* are with you, you will have what you request of Allah, and you will be able to do what Allah requests of you." *Dua* are said at all ritual and religious meetings and at meetings called to resolve disputes. They may be uttered aloud by a head *marabout* or whispered under the breath by each man at the meeting. The following is a typical *dua* used at an infant's naming ceremony: "Allah grant the baby life. Allah grant him luck. Allah heal his bodily ills. Allah grant that he be faithful to Islam. Allah protect him from the ill wishes of others. If Allah wishes. If He wishes. In the name of the prophet." *Dua* are also used as everyday greetings between individuals. To say "good night" or "good day," a Mandinko uses the *dua* "Allah grant you night" or "Allah give you day."

If the issue of vocabulary is set aside, the Arabic imprint on Mandinka religion

Missera: The mosque with thatched roof and surrounding palisade fence.

is less obvious for beliefs related to the durable aspects of the body and to their transmission through the burial period into the afterlife. Such beliefs appear to be more Mandinka and less Arabic. A human is composed of four main elements—flesh or body, breath, intelligence, and soul. The enduring parts of the human being are intelligence and soul; these go into the afterlife. Informants agree on the location of the two qualities. "Intelligence is located in the heart." "Soul is located all over the body." The Mandinka word "to die," *fa*, also means "to kill," implying that one never dies a so-called natural death. It is also believed that "whenever anyone dies he shall rise again." One's intelligence and soul will endure, and "one's body will rejoin them at the end of the world."

The transition into afterlife is orderly. At death a Mandinko becomes a sort of transitional corpse that is not entirely dead. The corpse is ritually washed shortly after death. This is done on a palm mat over a hole to collect the water, thought to be contaminated and capable of causing sickness if touched. The body is dressed in white burial clothes and is sewn into a white burial shroud, a practice characteristic of orthodox Islam. When a person dies during the day, burial must take place before sunset. A person who dies at night may be buried that same night. However, he is often not buried until the following morning to permit relatives and friends in other villages to attend the funeral.

There is no word for "funeral" other than *munko*, the name of the ceremonial rice bread distributed to the men at ritual meetings. The men conduct the funeral; the women do not participate directly, although they gather in the women's quarter nearest the funeral. Wrapped temporarily in a palm mat, the shrouded body is placed in the common ground near the deceased's house or in the village square. After the eulogy, uttered by a senior *marabout*, the *imam* places himself between the body and several rows of men standing for the pronouncement of final prayers.

Mankono Ba: Led by their imam, *the elders of the village solemnly face the east and say final prayers over the shrouded body of a woman.*

The body is propped to face the east, and the men face the east. In Arabic the *imam* repeats the phrase "Allah is great" several times. The men then carry the corpse on a bamboo mat held at shoulder level, and walk single file to the burial site. The women remain at the edge of the village and wail. Informants stressed the importance of protecting a corpse from the "contamination of dirt." They used this idea to justify the palm mat, the bamboo mat, the elevated transportation of the corpse, and at least in part, the need for a burial shroud. Without these protective measures "the corpse would be weakened during the forty-day period of judgment by the angel Malika and his two assistants Munkary and Wulakera." In Pakao, "Malika" is usually considered to be the personal name of the chief angel, while in Arabic it is literally the word for "angel."

The corpse is buried resting on its right side, with the head facing east and the feet north. The phrase "Allah is great" is written in Arabic on the dirt wall of the grave by the senior *marabout* present. The grave is unmarked except for the fence built around the site to protect it from marauding animals and cannibal-witches. The men complete the burial with a *dua* and rejoin their elders who have remained at the funeral in the village. Rice bread, biscuits, and kola nuts are distributed to the gathering, and a final *dua* completes the funeral.

Mandinko say that their manner of burial is to facilitate questioning of the corpse by the angel Malika. The grave is shallow, about one and a half feet deep and only as long as the body. The grave is covered over with sticks neatly placed together and with grass, in order to keep out the dirt piled on top in a small

Dar Silamé: The village smith, Malamine Sagnan, carries the body of his infant son and prepares to hand it over the fence for burial. The fence is built to keep out the cannibal-witch. The crouching men murmur prayers.

mound. A space is thus formed within the grave, providing the body with "air to breathe." Once the corpse is placed in the grave, the burial shroud is untied at the head and the feet to accommodate the interviewing by Malika. The forty-day period of judgment is marked by three mortuary ceremonies, and then a person's intelligence and soul go to the appointed place in the afterlife. At this point the worldly remains are considered "merely dirt." It is interesting to note that some of the features of burial described above were recorded in the 1730s by Francis Moore (1738:129). He reported that a corpse was wrapped in a white cloth and buried in a shallow grave covered by sticks. The cloth suggests a Muslim burial. Moore does point out that the burial took place in a house, a practice not followed in Pakao today.

Turning now to the Mandinka concept of the afterlife, heaven, purgatory, and hell are closely associated with "above," "center," and "below." Heaven is thought to be in the sky and hell below the ground, but people are less certain about where purgatory is. "It is somewhere in between the two." One informant places heaven on the "fringe" of the known universe. He says that "heaven is beyond the stars, on the fringe, purgatory is in the clouds, and hell is like being in a hole." Typically, heaven is described as pleasurable. Mandinko say that "aging is absent" in heaven, and that "it contains all foods including sugar." Hell is "very painful" and consists of "nothing but fire." It is the place for nonbelievers. Purgatory lies on the borders of heaven and hell. It exists "because hell is much too dangerous to border directly on heaven." Purgatory is a place "to take a breather." "A little bit of the prosperity of heaven is to be found in it." The Mandinka concept of purgatory appears to be essentially an indulgent concept, and its main purpose is to get at least some people out of hell and into heaven. One is never assigned directly to purgatory in the afterlife; this is theoretically impossible, according to the informants. Malika assigns a deceased either to heaven or hell directly. After a period of time the least evil people in hell are allowed into purgatory. One *marabout* informant thus describes the system of afterlife as "two paths and three layers."

Mandinka ideas of morality parallel their concept of the afterlife. Good deeds, deriving from good will, assure that one will go to heaven. Sin, caused by ill-will, increases the likelihood of being sent to hell. Mandinko say that heaven is a place of truth and righteousness, while hell is synonymous with lies and wrongdoing. Purgatory is characterized by penitence. One *marabout* explains that "there are seven wells on the border of hell and purgatory." "A sinner who repents can be forgiven by Allah and permitted to wash in the seven wells." Only then can Allah allow the sinner into purgatory. Another *marabout* speaks of "seven houses of hell with terrible suffering." A person who is sent to the lower six is condemned to remain in hell forever. If sent to the upper house, he is allowed by Allah into purgatory and from there eventually into heaven. Purgatory is thus associated with forgiveness and is consistent with a generally benevolent attitude among the Mandinko toward human shortcomings. Negative terms for "sin," "wrong," or "lie" do exist in the language, but they are rarely used in conversation. Instead, it is said with discreet understatement that someone "is not truthful" or that "his good deeds are insufficient."

3 / Social principles

In this chapter, I have singled out for discussion the more important principles of social order. The list is not exhaustive, nor have I ranked the sections in terms of consecutive importance. The reader may even elect to include different principles and to build a different model, but the sections below do at least present a sense of the priorities as perceived in Pakao thought.

VILLAGE INDEPENDENCE

The idea that villages are independent of each other is very much a part of the social ethic of Pakao. The French explorer Hecquard observed 125 years ago that "each village forms a sort of republic, governed by an *imam*, directing religion, and by a chief in charge of dispensing justice" (1855:123–124). Hecquard's observation is still characteristic of Pakao villages. Their independence is equated in Pakao thought with the triumph of Islam in the nineteenth century, when a more centralized (and non-Muslim) system based on kingship was systematically destroyed by Muslim warriors. The absence of kingship (or implicitly, the relative autonomy of villages) is considered symbolic of the advanced nature of Islam in Pakao. As the Mandinko say, "Two kings we have not; Allah is our one and only king."

Articulate as they are about the absence of kingship in their society, Mandinko offer few insights about the social independence of their villages. This independence is so obvious after analysis that Mandinko must be "thinking" about it in subconscious ways. For example, the survey of Dar Silamé in 1972 showed that among 264 extant marriages, only twenty-five of the wives (9 percent) were from other villages. Intermarriage between even neighboring villages is relatively infrequent. The large size of Mandinka villages probably favors this trend, since the chances are increased that a man can find a wife in his home village.

Other features reinforce the autonomy of villages. There is no local political or jural authority greater than the scope of a village. This is the extent of the authority of both the chief and the *imam*. Witchcraft accusations often focus on a neighboring village rather than one's own, and suspicions can run high between villages. Some informants claimed that drought in recent years had reinforced isolation, making it difficult, for example, to invite many outsiders from other villages to circumcision feasts. Within a sedentary system, villages are also respectful of each other's agricultural territory. The few land disputes in recent times resulted from the establishment of new villages, usually by non-Mandinka refugees from the war in Guinea-Bissau.

Despite the tendency of villages to stay out of each other's affairs, they do have limited contacts. Two villages will occasionally pool their labor to weed the forest paths that connect them. After a fire in one village, its neighbors rushed to its aid, bringing food and helping to rebuild. Small delegations of kinfolk also travel to other villages to attend rituals relating to birth, death, marriage, and circumcision.

TERRITORIAL SPACE AND LINEAGE

The Mandinko think of land around villages as a concentric matrix. The village itself is called "the place of houses" (*suokono*). The "peanut and millet fields" (*kungkoto*) surround the village in a band ranging from about one-half to one mile wide. "Rice fields" (*faroto*) are found on lower ground that often lies at the outer fringe of peanut and millet fields. Beyond the rice fields is "the forest" (*ulokono*). There are two important oppositions in this concentric classification of land. The first is geographic. The word for "forest" can also be used to mean "all the land beyond the confines of the village." This area, *ulokono*, is contrasted with *suokono*, so that to a Mandinko, a man is either in the village or in the peanut and millet fields/forest. The second pairing is based on sex. The forest and the peanut/millet fields are associated with men. The men farm peanuts and millet and as hunters venture into the forest. The male circumcision lodge is located in the fields. Women in turn are linked with the village and the rice fields. The seclusion of girls after circumcision takes place in the village. If asked the whereabouts of a certain woman, Mandinko normally reply either that she is in the village or in the rice fields.

Mandinko think of lineages in terms of territory. Each lineage is led or "commanded" by the eldest male. A minimal lineage is referred to as a "household" and contains the houses of a man and his immediate family. The next larger, minor lineage is called a "subhamlet," including the houses of genealogical brothers and their families. The houses of a subhamlet usually enclose a definite space. The men own and farm their fields as subhamlet groups. A women's quarter houses the wives and daughters of men in the subhamlet and contains the cookhouses. The women of a subhamlet farm the rice fields owned by the men of that subhamlet.

The "hamlet" is the next largest residential unit in a village and is correlated with a major lineage. Ideally, a hamlet contains within a specific area the houses of men of the same clan name. The five hamlets of Dar Silamé tend to be located in this ideal fashion. The men of a hamlet attend ritual meetings together, and walk to these meetings lined up behind the head man, roughly according to the seniority of their ages. The hamlet also defines an exogamous group. The men of one hamlet must give their daughters in marriage to the men of another hamlet.

Of course there are exceptions to the ideal, and these are outlined briefly. In

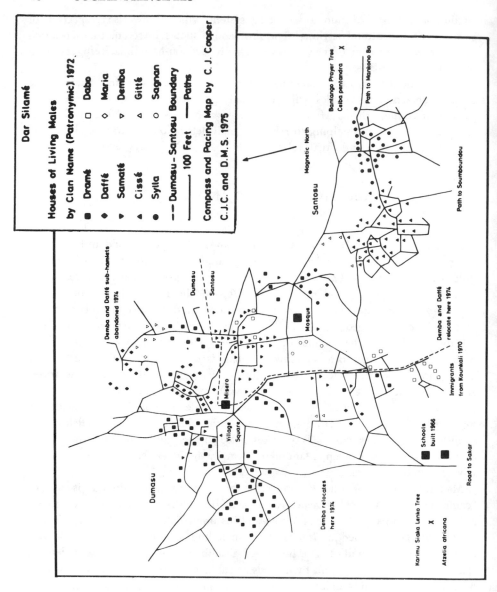

both Mankono Ba and Soumboundou the large chiefly lineages, Sagnan and Camera respectively, live in several hamlets. Each of these hamlets attends ritual meetings as a distinct group. In the context of marriage, however, all of the Sagnan of Mankono Ba act together as one exogamous group. In Soumboundou this is not so. Each Camera hamlet acts as a separate exogamous group and is able thus to marry girls of other Camera hamlets. Another variation of hamlet rules is found in Dar Silamé. There, the Sylla attend meetings with the Cissé, demonstrating that the two act as a single hamlet in the political sense. Sylla and Cissé act as separate hamlets in the exogamous sense and are thus able to marry each other's girls.

In keeping with the notion of village independence, a lineage ceases to have

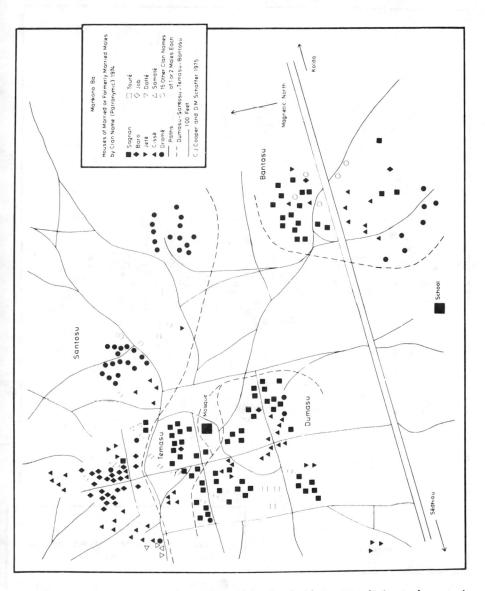

any functional importance above the village level. If the Mandinko had a maxi-
mal lineage, it would theoretically include members of the same clan from
different villages. The Mandinko do have a concept of land that can serve as a
basis of organization among the hamlets within a village. This is the widely used
notion of "upper village" (*santosu*) and "lower village" (*dumasu*), constituting
a bifurcated division in all Pakao villages. The division is identified on accompanying village maps. Explaining the division, some Mandinka informants said
that it refers literally to the higher and lower ground in a village. The slight
difference in elevation can be perceived only during the rainy season via the
drainage of water. In practice, the two divisions of the village often act as

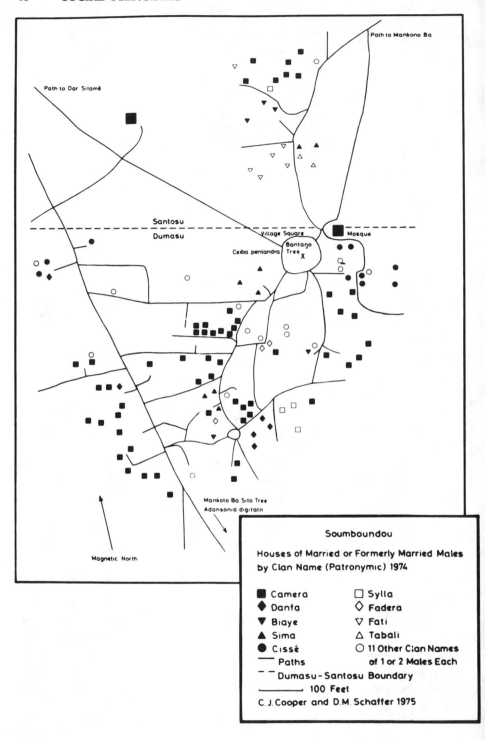

Path to Mankono Ba

Path to Dar Silamé

Santosu

Dumasu

Village Square

Ceiba pentandra

Bantaŋo
Tree
X

Mosque

Mankoto Ba Sito Tree
Adansonia digitata

Magnetic North

Soumboundou

Houses of Married or Formerly Married Males
by Clan Name (Patronymic) 1974

■ Camera   □ Sylla
◆ Danfa   ◇ Fadera
▼ Biaye   ▽ Fati
▲ Sima   △ Tabali
● Cissé   ○ 11 Other Clan Names
— Paths   of 1 or 2 Males Each
- - Dumasu–Santosu Boundary
————— 100 Feet
C. J. Cooper and D. M. Schaffer 1975

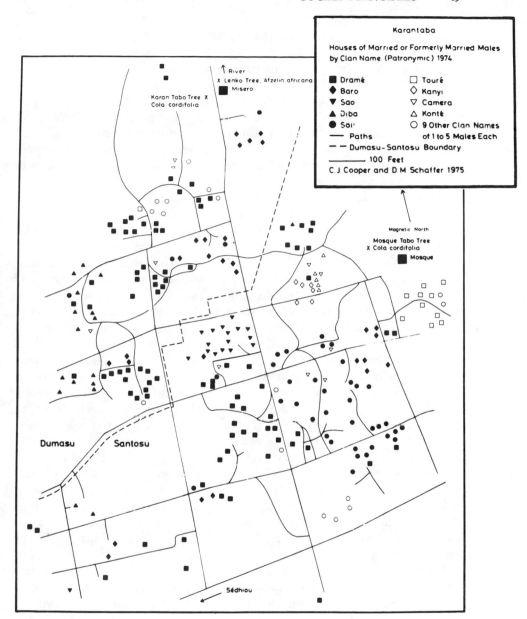

Karantaba

Houses of Married or Formerly Married Males by Clan Name (Patronymic) 1974

■ Dramé   □ Touré
♦ Baro   ◇ Kanyı
▼ Sao   ▽ Camera
▲ Dıba   △ Konté
● Saı'   ○ 9 Other Clan Names
—— Paths   of 1 to 5 Males Each
— — Dumasu-Santosu Boundary
——————— 100 Feet
C J Cooper and D M Schaffer 1975

↑ River
X Lenko Tree, Afzelia africana
■ Misero

Karan Tabo Tree X
Cola cordifolia

Magnetic North

Mosque Tabo Tree
X Cola cordifolia
■ Mosque

Dumasu   Santosu

Sédhiou

political groups, competing for the positions of chief and *imam* and creating a source of opposition. Upper and lower villages may build separate circumcision lodges, and the distinction also figures in the organization of age-sets.[1] Some informants claim that historically the bifurcation in a village delineates two original hamlets that exchanged and still exchange women in marriage.

[1] The large village of Mankono Ba had two further divisions, "center village" and "outer village." Like upper and lower village, these divisions can figure in age organization, the circumcision ritual, and political rivalry.

CROSS-COUSIN

Sanao (cross-cousin) has an importance in Pakao society not only as the relative who is preferred in marriage, but as a concept of alliance. The most basic usage of *sanao* is as a kinship term. It means either the matrilateral cross-cousin, who is preferred in marriage from the male perspective, or the patrilateral cross-cousin, who is preferred from the female perspective. The Pakao Mandinko thus have what is called a preferential system of matrilateral cross-cousin marriage. Informants stress the importance of *sanao* as a kinship term by pointing to its derivation from *asan*, meaning either "to buy" or "to sell." The etymology is significant, since marriage is a profoundly economic transaction (see Chapter 5). Informants also see an etymological similarity between *sanao* and the word for gold, *sano*.

While referring to cross-cousin as its primary sense, the term *sanao* can have broader implications in Mandinka society. It can mean "hamlet ally" in the sense of an alliance between two hamlets within a village, based on the exchange of cross-cousins in marriage. Beyond the confines of a single village, *sanao* can also refer to a clan with whom another clan has joking relations. As in the case of "cross-cousin," these secondary meanings of *sanao* imply unity and mutuality.

Hamlet allies are said in the local idiom to be "one and the same." The mutual obligation of this alliance can be a dominant force in village politics. The *sanao* alliance of Sylla and Cissé hamlets is one example discussed in several places in the remainder of this book. I found at least one pair of *sanao* hamlets in Karantaba, Dar Silamé, Mankono, and Soumboundou.[2] In the first three villages, the *sanao* alliance is attributed to a relation of mother's brother and sister's son between the founders of the two hamlets. In each of the three villages, one of the paired hamlets lies in "upper village" and the other lies in "lower village." An elder of Mankono Ba, Arfanba Sagnan, explained this arrangement by recalling a legend in which his village was originally composed of two hamlets, the chiefly Sagnan and the Cissé, lying in lower and upper village and exchanging women in marriage. This line of thought suggests that the classification of upper and lower village may have arisen to distinguish two original village hamlets linked by marriage exchange.

The final sense of *sano* refers to a system of joking reactions between two clans whenever they are found. Some well-known clan names paired in these relations are Sagnan (Keita)/Touré, Manjan/Dramé, and Dramé/Jeta. I recorded a myth for each pair explaining that the latter clan had once been the totem of the former and was avoided by it maritally. Eventually, "totemic relations were succeeded by joking relations" that permitted marriage. According to one of the myths, this change was brought about when a starving Sagnan was fed by a generous Touré with flesh from his thigh, and the two agreed to become friends thereafter.

---

[2] Examples of *sanao* hamlets are Dramé/Samaté and Sylla/Cissé in Dar Silamé; Dramé/Diba in Karantaba; Sagnan/Cissé and Sagnan/Dramé in Mankono Ba; Camera/Cissé and Camera/Biaye in Soumboundou.

CHIEF AND *IMAM*

The separation of secular and religious authority in the positions of chief and *imam* is a fundamental of village organization. The chief convenes and presides over meetings of the village elders to settle disputes involving, among other things, theft, land ownership, damage to crops caused by livestock, the jurisdiction of district authorities, the performance of a schoolteacher, and the election of the village *imam*. The principal duty of the *imam* is to lead prayers at mosque.

It is also true that the fairly sharp distinction between chief and *imam* exists mainly in the contrast of their principal duties. In the context of this particularly religious society, the two men who hold these positions can rival each other in influence, and their powers can overlap. A chief such as Majima Dramé was considered a distinguished *marabout* in his own right, and his religious standing as a healer and counselor was significant. The chiefly Dramé of Karantaba and Dar Silamé have many fine *marabouts* in their midst. Chief Fodé Alemamé Dramé of Karantaba actually led prayers at mosque during the *imam's* illness. In Dar Silamé, the Dramé resent claims that Sylla, the descendants of Syllaba, are "all *marabouts*," and so the two hamlets rival each other in religious matters. A second source of conflict between chief and *imam* lies in the nature of the *imam's* election. Unlike chieftainship, which is restricted to one founding hamlet, the position of *imam* is open to all religious elders who are freemen (that is, not slaves). The hamlets vie for the position, creating a political event occasionally so divisive that only a chief can resolve it. The election process brings the religious position very much into the world of secular politics. There is a third, equally political source of conflict between the two positions. Both the chief and *imam* have their natural constituencies in the same village. The *imam's* ability to control a following has sometimes outstripped that of the chief. In Dar Silamé, villagers still debate whether this was true of at least one Sylla *imam* named Fodali.[3] The competition between chief and *imam* is intensified because both positions are considered roughly equivalent in prestige, if opposite in nature.

One basis for the difference between chief and *imam* is in the principle of eligibility. It is said that "the village founder provides the chief" and that this founding lineage "walks the land" in the sense of ownership and command. Because of their pervasiveness, the Dramé clan are said to own (walk) Pakao. Ideally, the position of *imam* should not remain indefinitely in the chiefly hamlet, but should circulate over time among several hamlets. One informant explained that the position of *imam* is a power to be given away by the chiefly hamlet to other hamlets as part of the social contract. "When you clear land to found a village, you do not become *imam*, even if you are instructed in the Koran. You must give it to someone else. Even if this other person is your stranger, as your coresident he must be chosen. If he is wise in the Koran, he must become *imam*."

An examination of succession to the position of *imam* turned up two trends. In several villages, the *imams* had been chosen from some three or more hamlets,

---

[3] For more about Fodali Sylla, see Chapter 5.

supporting the theoretical notion of a circulating position. One apparent exception was Karantaba, where for reasons of religious antiquity only the founding Dramé lineage provided the *imams*. In Karantaba, however, the Dramé are dispersed in several hamlets, so that even in this instance *imams* have been chosen from more than one hamlet. A second trend was also found in several villages, where despite the circulation of the position, it tended to be confined to one, nonchiefly hamlet. Significant examples are the Sylla of Dar Silamé and Ouducari and the Dramé of Mankono Ba. Each family has a long history of religious specialization and includes numerous *marabouts* in its ranks. There is perhaps an obvious potential for conflict between such religiously influential families and the chiefly hamlet. One of the best examples is in Dar Silamé.

Dramé resentment of Sylla's religious prestige has smoldered for years. The first Sylla *imam* was Fodali, a son of *jihad* leader Syllaba and remembered in Pakao for his resistance to colonial pacification at the beginning of the twentieth century. Fodali's eldest son Fodé Lamine served as deputy *imam*, but died before election to the full position. Fodali's three younger sons, Karamo, Thierna, and Sancoun, later succeeded each other as *imams*. The election of Sancoun in 1971 ignited a furor among the Dramé and nearly caused part of the village to secede.

On his deathbed, the popular Thierna Sylla named as his successor deputy *imam* Arfan Sanji Cissé. Arfan Sanji disqualified himself during electoral meetings of the village elders and threw his support to Sancoun Sylla. Arfan Sanji's mother was a Sylla, and three of his wives were Sylla. He did not consider it appropriate to take precedence over Sancoun, who in a classificatory sense was both his "mother's brother" and "father-in-law." The Dramé detested Sancoun and put up a rival candidate for the position, Fodé Kemo Dramé, a *marabout* whose father had been *imam*. A number of reasons were given for Sancoun's unpopularity. A difficult man, he was not on speaking terms with Thierna and never attended mosque during the latter's tenure as *imam*. Sancoun snubbed Samaté hamlet by refusing to let his daughter marry a Samaté whom he considered to have an inferior knowledge of the Koran. Dramé were also convinced that the Sylla had too strong a hold on the position of *imam*. Fodé Kemo Dramé tried to persuade the *imam* of a neighboring village to visit Dar Silamé and resolve the election in his favor. The Dramé considered taking over the position permanently, and Fodé Kemo argued to this effect. Arfan Sanji Cissé consistently refused to yield to Dramé pressure that he become *imam* as a compromise candidate. He sent a message to Dramé saying that "Sylla are all *marabouts*, the sons of Syllaba; they must be *imam* before anyone else." At a final elders' meeting Cissé threatened, "Unless you name Sancoun *imam*, Cissé and Sylla will secede, name a new chief and *imam*, build a new mosque, and become a new village." At that point chief Fodé Ibrahima Dramé intervened and summarily declared Sancoun the new *imam*. Sancoun remained bitter. In 1973, he left Dar Silamé with some of his followers and founded the village of Taiba about four miles away. Arfan Sanji Cissé became the new *imam* of Dar Silamé. The affair certainly illustrates the political nature of election to religious office. It also demonstrates some of the political power that an *imam* can wield. The Mandinko have not successfully founded a village in the Pakao area for some 100 years. Sancoun took an unusual step in doing so, and of course by founding Taiba, he became its first chief.

The rules of succession to chieftainship make this office appear more restrictive than the *imam*, even predetermined. The chief is normally the eldest free member of the founding lineage, while the *imam* can come from any hamlet and, though an elder, is not necessarily the oldest *marabout* in a village. Yet the Mandinko have ways of adjusting the rules of chiefly succession and succeed in contesting even this position. Citing his poor health, the Dramé convinced Bakary Fanta to declare himself ineligible as a successor to a deceased chief. The Dramé then "elected" Majima, who was Bakary's more popular younger brother. Ironically, Bakary is said to have regained his health, outlived Majima, and even succeeded him as chief. Another way that subhamlets compete for chieftainship within their hamlet is to summon an elder kinsman to return home from another village. Since *marabouts* and other Mandinko travel frequently, it is not difficult to find an emigrant who would be the eldest member of the chiefly lineage if only he could be persuaded to return home. In Mankono Ba, three of the last four chiefs were selected in this way. Chieftainship can circulate among the subhamlets of the chiefly hamlet (which is always the largest in a village) the way the position of *imam* circulates among the hamlets of the whole village. The electoral process can thus foster both dissent and integration among lineages. In the nineteenth century, chiefs made decisions of peace or war, and *imams* were concerned with the militant advance of Islam. In the absence of such weighty tasks in the twentieth century, the election of chiefs and *imams* provides one of the more important dramas in village life.

The Mandinko expect virtuous conduct on the part of their leaders, and are able to impeach them and, if necessary, remove them from office. During my stay in Mankono, the chief was accused by fellow villagers of embezzling money entrusted to him on behalf of the peanut farmers cooperative. After several heated debates, an angry group of elders temporarily took away the chief's *tabala*, a summoning drum emblematic of his authority.[4] The Mandinko can also idealize their leaders and have built up a mythological lore about them. Great age and Koranic wisdom are the virtues most readily associated with an *imam*. The Mandinko also find that religious virtues are consistent with being a good chief. Fodé Ibrahima Dramé illustrated this for me with a comment about Majima: "Wherever he went, he was followed by a crowd. No one knew injustice in him except for the waiting required when he prayed. He was indefatigable and could hunt in the forest day and night. He enjoyed laughter and amusement and was wise toward everyone. He never hid wealth in his trunk, and he gave nearly everything to the needy."

KANDA

Mandinka ideas about democracy and leadership are not strictly defined in terms of chief and *imam*. There is in the society a relatively influential person who could be called a self-made man. This is the *kanda*. Mandinko say that a man is a *kanda* "when he has a large family, several sons and fields, a lot of money, and an influence greater than a chief or *imam*." The definition of a *kanda* once included

---

[4] The emblem of the *imam*'s authority is a staff which hangs in the front (eastern side) of the mosque, next to the *imam*'s place when leading prayers.

the ownership of several slaves. However, it is important to the contemporary Mandinka concept of democracy that a slave can also become a *kanda*. In Dar Silamé, a slave named Bitori purchased his freedom and became a *kanda* during the early part of this century.

Kanda is an egalitarian concept because any successful entrepreneur can assume the role. The position is also controversial because it implies superior wealth and position. A man thought to be a *kanda* would never use the word to describe himself for fear of alienating other villagers. The term was used in public only rarely. For example, someone who gave too much money at a meeting of the elders might be teased that he was "acting like a *kanda*."

There is one formal sense of *kanda* found only in Mankono Ba. There, the *kanda* is always the second oldest freeman in the chiefly lineage. In Mankono, this *kanda* is a sort of peacemaker and alternative power to the chief or *imam*, much as the informal *kanda* would be in other villages. These informal *kanda* were also to be found in Mankono Ba. Arfanba Sagnan held no formal office but in terms of his wealth in land, houses, and cattle, and because of a strong personality, he was clearly the most influential man in the village. He of course vigorously denied the title when I questioned him about it and said the only *kanda* was Lam Binta Sagnan, the one formal *kanda* of Mankono. Arfanba's influence revealed itself in several ways. At 73, he was a classificatory grandson of the chief, but easily dominated him by strength of personality. During important meetings Arfanba sat by the chief and aided him with argument and counsel. The chief was hesitant to speak about oral history and called on Arfanba instead, because no one knew as much or spoke so eloquently. It was Arfanba who intervened in a dispute between the chief and a Sagnan youth who wanted to build a house. The chief refused to have another dwelling in his subhamlet and had threatened to push it down. Once Arfanba persuaded the elder Sagnan to calm down, the grateful youth went ahead with construction. During the embezzling incident, Arfanba also convinced the other village elders that the chief should not be deposed. The men who took the summoning drum away in fact gave it to Lam Binta Sagnan, the formal *kanda* whom many villagers favored as the new chief. Arfanba appealed during an elders' meeting that the rules of succession should not be broken and successfully pleaded that the chief be forgiven.

The Senegalese Foreign Minister once visited Mankono Ba, and villagers complained bitterly to him about the system for distributing grain during the drought relief effort. Arfanba was enraged that the villagers could be so ungrateful, and after lashing out at them, walked out of the meeting. He returned only after the Foreign Minister cajoled him, apologized for the villagers, and, indeed, called Arfanba his "host," a title of respect.

THE POWER OF ELDERS

In addition to the chief, *imam*, and *kanda*, there is a more populous class of leadership in Mandinka society—the elders. Both male and female elders have great jural authority. Someone's status as an elder is an informal concept that

Dar Silamé: An elder woman and her grandsons.

grows with age relative to other surviving elders. One of the most visible privileges of the status among men is the right to sit with the elders' council. This is the group of elders who occupy the central place at all meetings.[5] An authorization among elder women is the right to say prayers outside the palisade enclosure around the mosque.

The authority of elders operates because of the deep respect held for them by younger people. Respect is inculcated from an early age and is one of the most emphatic themes of the circumcision songs sung by male novices during seclusion. The novices sing, for example, "If an elder tells you something, you must never answer with disrespect." Women point out that a major objective of girls' circumcision is similarly to teach the novice "to respect and to obey her elder."

Ultimately, the source of the male elder's power can be traced to Islam, to his senior position in the mosque, and to his prayers (*dua*) believed capable of life and death. One way the young men acknowledge this power is by giving alms to the senior men in return for a *dua*. For example, the students of Mankono sought a *dua* by stacking firewood as alms inside the mosque enclosure. They asked the elders to pray for their success in school. The *dua* of an elder may also have a dangerous effect. One youth from Dar Silamé returned money he had stolen from us soon after the elders threatened at mosque to have him rendered insane by a Manjak pagan. In Karantaba a young man died for a similar reason. "He had stolen, and the elders of the mosque had asked Allah to ruin his life." The curse allegedly caused him to go insane for three years and then killed him.

SEX DISTINCTION

Mandinko draw a sharp distinction between the sexes at the level of thought. Men consider women uneducated, pagan, and stronger than themselves. Their greater strength is said to be associated with their buttocks and arms, which are developed through hours of pounding a pestle every day. It is also said that "a man's strength is in his right arm and that a woman's is in her left." Men think of themselves as Muslim and more intelligent. A man's strength is associated with his neck and thighs. Men also think women like to make love too much.

Women, in turn, think men are stronger, and consider any mention of their own arms and buttocks a grave insult. They believe that "a woman's left arm is more powerful than her right." They agree for the most part with the male contention that women are pagan, even though prayers are faithfully uttered by both sexes five times daily.

The differences between men and women at a conceptual level parallel distinctions in the division of labor. These pervade Mandinka life, dividing up the agricultural roles and relegating the domestic duties to women and permitting men alone the use of the mosque building. Women believe that they do more physical labor than men, and I heard some of them complain that "Mandinka

---

[5] More is said of this council and the elders as a class in the final chapter. See the section on age organization in Chapter 5.

Mankono Ba: Synchronizing their efforts, three girls separate millet from the chaff by pounding.

women work too much." The workload among women is especially strenuous during summer because not only does it consist of year-round duties such as cooking, caring for children, and washing clothes, but includes rice farming as well. To keep the washing and drinking jugs full, women carry heavy buckets of water, balanced on their heads, several times daily.

The division of labor extends to ritual activity. All aspects of the separate circumcision rites are closely guarded secrets kept by the sexes from each other. The novices are carefully warned that they will be cursed by their elders (of the same sex) if they tell a circumcision secret. The men and women also divide up

Soumboundou: Babu Siman, wife of our host, chief Jeta Camera, makes clay pots. Well-water kept in such pots stays cool and becomes more potable after the silt sinks to the bottom.

duties relating to burial. The women ritually wash the effects of a deceased person, regardless of the sex. The corpse itself is washed and dressed by members of the same sex. For females this is performed by the queen or other elder women, and for males it is done by senior *marabouts*. The men conduct the funeral for either sex and then bury the body.

The ritual distinction of the sexes implies something of a structural equivalence. There is a separate circumcision ceremony for both sexes, and the two also have important roles to play in the preparations for each burial. The ritual distinctions based on sex are also an indication of the suspicion that exists between men and women. Mandinko believe that people are attacked by cannibal-witches of the opposite sex and that their vulnerability to these witches increases during rites of passage.

WOMEN'S ORGANIZATION

Women in Mandinka society are highly organized, and it would not be an exaggeration to say that "village" positions such as chief and *imam* operate within an essentially male system and have little direct relevance for the lives of women. The dominant figure in women's organization is the circumcision queen, or simply "queen" (*musomansa*) as she is called in Mandinko. Her power derives from her control of the women's ritual apparatus in a village. Her most significant ritual

Mankono Ba: In the seclusion of a rice field pond, the elder women ritually wash the clothes of a deceased some two hours after burial.

duties include convening girls' circumcision and supervising the ritual itself and subsequent seclusion. The queen is usually the acknowledged village expert on washing the dead and the effects of the dead. She is a knowledgeable midwife, and the women consult her routinely for advice on health, medicine, and the raising of children.

Queens tend to be members of the artisan–praise-singer caste, even in villages dominated by nobles. In the four villages where my fieldwork was concentrated, I also recorded as queens one noble incumbent and two women, deceased in recent years, who were of the slave caste. Generally speaking, queens are thought to be wizards, capable of perceiving evil cannibal-witches and of transforming into animal shapes to combat them if necessary. At least among nobles, it is thought that wizards are concentrated among artisan–praise singers. This association may be one explanation for the preponderance of this caste among the ranks of queens. The queen's alleged power as a wizard probably accounts most for her reputation as a dangerous person. The queen's authority is quite visible during circumcision and is summed up well in a song sung by the novices: "My grandmother, my grandmother, you are the post in the middle of the lodge."

During the circumcision ceremony, attended by the women of the village, the queen is assisted by a circumcisor and by an informal entourage of elder women. Like the queen, the circumcisor is often a wizard and tends to be from the artisan–praise-singer caste. On rare occasions the queen plays the role of circumcisor herself.

Kinship is one factor favoring the emergence of a particular woman as queen. In one case, involving Koto Fadera of Dar Silamé and Sanji Fadera of Bani, two genealogical sisters were queens. Affinal kinship is also important in determining who becomes queen. It is not unusual for a queen to be married to a male cir-cumcisor. Kéluntan Sagnan, the husband of Koto Fadera, was a circumcisor. His father and mother were, in their own time, male circumcisor and queen of Dar Silamé. Ba Tabali, the queen of Soumboundou, was similarly married to a cir-cumcisor. Queens tend to have a prominent deputy who is a likely successor. When Koto Fadera died she was succeeded by her younger cowife Kady Sumaré. The new queen is elected by general acclamation among village women, and she might hold a feast for the women as a demonstration of her new role. Once she has convened and supervised a circumcision, her position is established.

Another women's society is composed of *dembajasa*. Literally, the term means "clowning mother," and there is an association of some ten to fifty of these women in every Pakao village, depending on the size of the village. Typically, a woman becomes a *dembajasa* after two or three of her infants have died. She hopes that this change in her status will magically cause future offspring to be spared by evil spirits. One colorful aspect of the *dembajasa's* role is to perform a transvestite dance in male trousers and shirts, and with a pointedly absurd headdress made of a gourd helmet decorated with beads or bottle tops suspended from it. The women dance on the day of boys' circumcision or on a day of feasting hosted by their leader. The leader of the *dembajasa* is elected by acclamation.

When a woman becomes a *dembajasa*, she permanently adopts new given and clan names. These are easily identified with a neighboring ethnic group, usually one considered to be non-Muslim. The given names are sometimes the name of the ethnic group itself and include Bainunko, Jola, Manjako, Balanto, and Fulo. Only the last one is typically Muslim. The naming practice of *dembajasa* is viewed with disfavor by men, who consider it inconsistent with Islam and even insulting. They refer derisively to *dembajasa* as "silly fools." Women, in contrast, carefully respect the new names chosen by the *dembajasa* and use them routinely.[6] The naming procedure initially caused confusion in my genealogical work, because *dembajasa* were calling themselves by a name other than the one used by their husbands.

There is a certain tension, even resistance, in the *dembajasa* system with refer-ence to Islam. Two elder women speculated that the system might have arisen among groups of non-Muslim women enslaved during the nineteenth century *jihad*. However, the only widely used explanation of the system was the desire to ensure the survival of future children. *Dembajasa* strongly believe in their method's potential for success, and there is ample evidence to prove them right. Sanjiba Dramé, the wife of my host in Dar Silamé, became a *dembajasa* after her first four infants died. Her next four children, all sons, grew to manhood. Becoming a *dembajasa* does not detract from a woman's reputation and can enhance it. The queens of both Mankono and Soumboundou were *dembajasa*.

---

[6] The men know the *dembajasa* name of a woman and will provide it if asked. They prefer to call *dembajasa* women by the names given them at birth.

Soumboundou: A dembajasa, *wearing her gourd headdress and a man's shirt, performs her dance.*

There are additional means of social organization among women. The women (like the men) are organized into age-sets headed by an overall leader. The women's age-sets are important in rice cultivation and are led by a powerful woman sometimes called a "chosen mother." A queen, a circumcisor, or a head of the *dembajasa* association or some other woman of importance can be called a "women's *kanda*" honorifically. In Mankono Ba there is a rule formalizing the selection of the women's *kanda*. The title is held by the two eldest women of the chiefly Sagnan hamlet. Like the less formal women's *kanda* in other villages, these two women play a leadership role by hosting feasts and serving as advisors on women's affairs.

CASTE

In contemporary Pakao there are three castes: noble, artisan–praise-singer, and slave. The artisan–praise-singer category is subdivided into smiths, leatherworkers, and praise-singers. There are four types of praise-singers: *fino* and *joka*, and *kora* and *balafong* musicians, all of which are explained below. The caste system has an effect on several aspects of the society, and is perhaps best understood by focusing on each one of them.

Marriage   The three castes are rigorously observed endogamous groups outside of which it is not ordinarily possible to marry. There are exceptions, however. In recent times a few marriages have taken place between slaves and members of other castes. In the last two or three generations, the more frequent combination involved a noble man and a slave woman. I recorded only one case where both partners were still living. Less often, a noble girl is permitted to marry a slave if his owner is willing to set him free.

A contemporary example of such a marriage also serves to illustrate how a slave can be ritually freed. In 1966, a slave man named Keluntan Gitté wished to marry a noble girl. After protracted negotiations, he was allowed to pay his owner, Arfan Sanji Cissé, a sum of $16 (4000 CFA), called "freedom money." This is a sizable amount of money for a Pakao farmer, who considers himself lucky if he earns more than $100 annually. Arfan Sanji, the headman of Cissé hamlet, had inherited the ownership of Keluntan along with the other members of his Gitté subhamlet. To accept the freedom money, Arfan Sanji hosted a ceremonial meeting attended by the men of Dar Silamé. In front of Arfan Sanji's house, Keluntan's head was shaved, and he was pronounced free by his former owner. The meeting was concluded with *dua* and the distribution of rice dough.

Hierarchy   At least some Mandinko believe that the caste system implies rank. Nobles consider themselves at the top of the scale. The nobles of Dar Silamé and Mankono Ba have quite a condescending attitude toward the artisans and praise-singers who predominate in Soumboundou. Keba Dramé told me that he has no friends in Soumboundou and has never spent the night there. Several nobles of Mankono accused Soumboundou of harboring dangerous cannibal-witches. The nobles also derisively called the villagers of Soumboundou "our artisan–praise-singers," referring to a patron–client relation that existed in prior times.

Most Mandinko also rank slaves lowest in the caste system. Mandinko are sensitive about this caste and rarely talk about it. In public, villagers avoid mentioning who the slaves are. To call someone a slave to his face is the worst possible insult, and such a taunt has resulted in a savage fight.

The hierarchical attitudes described above are complemented by a strong feeling of egalitarianism among the castes that is a distinctive feature of the Mandinka system. The ownership of slaves has become somewhat fictitious because they

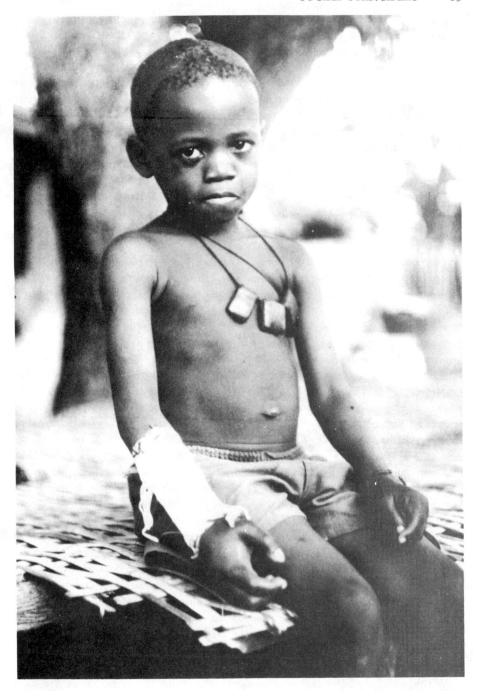

Soumboundou: Syrifu Danfa displays his broken arm, set the previous day by a Mandinka specialist in a neighboring village. The lightweight splint is made of bamboo strips tightly bound to the arm and is the traditional way of setting a broken limb.

now farm their own land and work for themselves. Slaves still technically have owners (who are the descendants of their ancestors' owners), but they are sometimes permitted to purchase their freedom. Slaves can also accumulate considerable wealth. Karafa Cissé of Dar Silamé owned a large herd of cattle and may well have been the richest man in the village. Slaves can be *marabouts*. They attend mosque side by side with the members of other castes and are equally devout Muslims. I think Islam has had much to do with creating a greater sense of equality between slaves and the other castes. Probably Islam also lies behind the attitude of artisan–praise-singers that they are equal, if not superior, to nobles. A survey of Soumboundou in 1974 showed that this opinion is widely held among the men and women in the village. One *marabout* in Soumboundou refused to rank the two castes. Picking up a glass jar, he said, "Man is like a bottle; his nature depends on what is inside." The *imam* of Soumboundou concluded that nobles were more important than artisan–praise-singers only after arguing that caste differences do not matter in the eyes of Islam: "The artisan–praise-singer and the noble do not exist in the Koran. They are like two old men, one scheming, represented by the artisan–praise-singer who, through flattery, robs the noble of all his goods. The noble is more important since he is the one who must give."

Place of Residence   Members of the three castes are distributed unequally. A few villages in Pakao and Suna were founded by artisan–praise-singers, are now dominated by members of this caste, and have no nobles at all. In these villages artisans and praise-singers provide the chief and *imam*. Noble villages such as Karantaba and Mankono Ba have no artisan–praise-singers. There are also examples of noble villages, such as Dar Silamé, which have at least one artisan–praise-singer lineage and are thus the only villages where all the castes are represented. In any noble village, however, only nobles may become chief or *imam*; members of the other two castes are ineligible. The tendency of one caste to dominate a village is favored by the Mandinka system of according chieftainship and original land ownership to the founding lineage. The endogamous nature of caste helps to facilitate the trend. Slaves are the most evenly distributed caste and are found in most, if not all, villages. Throughout the nineteenth century, great numbers of slaves were captured or purchased, accounting for the wide distribution of their descendants. In Pakao there are no examples of predominantly slave villages, and there are no reported instances of a slave's becoming a chief or *imam*.

Occupation   Today, the artisan–praise-singer is the only caste that may also be a profession. There is neither a noble nor a slave profession. Irrespective of caste, all able-bodied men do at least some farming. Caste imposes no theoretical limitation on who may become a *marabout*, although in practice the greatest number of *marabouts*, especially the more well-known, are of noble descent. The caste system has no occupational implication for women, except perhaps in determining who is more likely to become a village queen.

Within the caste of artisan–praise-singers, the smith is recognized as the most important occupation. Several informants rank this status higher than chief or imam. One man argues that "the smith is the most important because without him society falls apart." Working with the traditional bellows, charcoal, and iron scrap, he makes metal-tipped ploughs, axes, and other items. Most smiths are

Mankono Ba: Damura Sagnan makes a hole in an ax handle by pounding a red-hot spike through it. The ax-head, fashioned by a local smith, can then be inserted.

expert in repairing bicycles, and there is no shortage of business. Among artisan–praise-singers, the man born a smith is most likely to practice the trade.

The smith has a reputation for truthfulness and is likely to be a wizard. These qualities help to expand his role beyond that of making metal tools. The smith may be called on to distribute rice dough and kola nuts at ritual meetings, and he will sometimes serve as paymaster for the agricultural cooperative. Smiths broke up several fights during my fieldwork and are said to be peacemakers. A smith can be asked to relay the words of an important elder after mosque or during a eulogy. When a stranger visits a village and has no host, the smith is often the first to extend him an invitation. One of the smith's more important functions is to serve as a male circumcisor and lodge chief, although nobles and other members of the artisan–praise-singer caste sometimes perform these functions.

The leatherworker is generally considered less important than the smith. Few people born into this status actually practice the profession. Those who do report a thriving business, mostly concerned with preparing cases for written charms. A leatherworker often has a referral relationship with a particular *marabout*, guaranteeing a more predictable income and assuring the *marabout* that his charms will not be secretly copied and sold. When Talibo Dramé developed elephantiasis and could no longer farm a large field, he took up leather-making to supplement his income. Talibo's business thrived because of his friendship with the *marabout* Keba Dramé.

The praise-singer is a source of entertainment but is held in mild contempt because he incessantly demands money and because his musical arts are considered somewhat frivolous in the religious atmosphere that pervades the society. The Mandinko say that "one cannot sing and dance excessively and be a good Muslim." The low status of the praise-singer is illustrated by a proverb that Mandinko say among themselves jokingly: "When paid, the praise-singer sings well."

The prevalent and most popular type of praise-singer in Pakao is the *fino*. This is due partly to the large size of the chiefly Camera clan in Soumboundou, whose lineage was established by a *fino*. Smaller *fino* lineages live in a few other villages. The *fino* chants his praise, calling out honorific names and reciting lists of characters from the Koran. The latter chant is called *hadiso* and is probably from the Arabic *hadith*, a parable or narrative relating the words and deeds of the prophet. The *fino* performs at infants' naming ceremonies and occasionally leads client villagers to their prayer tree during Islamic festivals.

The proliferation of the *fino* in Pakao is one of the best examples of the adjustment to Islam that the Mandinko have made without losing a basic element of social structure—the position of the praise-singer in the caste system. In the late eighteenth century, Park noticed two types of praise-singers (1969:212–214). One he describes as "singing men," who "greatly outnumbered" the second sort of praise-singer—Islamic bards whose duties included "singing devout hymns and performing religious ceremonies." This second praise-singer described by Park resembles the modern *fino*. Today in Pakao the *fino* far outnumber the other more musical praise-singers known as "singing men" and whose numbers flourished during Park's time. The evidence suggests that Islam may have favored the expansion of the *fino's* ranks in society at the expense of other praise-singers. For example, today the *joka* has fallen into low regard by the elders of the mosque, and few people actually practice his art. The *joka* invents rhymed phrases and sings them accompanied by a drummer. There are almost no *kora* and *balafong* musicians still living in Pakao, and they are scarce in neighboring villages in middle Casamance. The *kora* is a stringed instrument with a large resonator made from a skin stretched over a gourd bowl. The *balafong* is a wooden xylophone with gourd resonators. Reputable *kora* and *balafong* players emigrate to cities and towns where they can earn more money.

4 / History

In the Pakao view of history, the first significant event is the founding of a village. There is no creation myth, nor a myth about the founding of Pakao as a whole. The absence of such concepts is merely viewed as proof of the country's antiquity. When questioned about the origin of Pakao, elders indignantly replied that "Pakao is eternal." They always use the same phrase to say this: *Bakao bada bada*. *Bada bada* is a local rendition of the Arabic *abadan abadan*, "forever and ever," and it connotes a deep religious significance in which great age is equated both to importance and to holiness.

When pressed hard, the elders will admit that Mandinka Muslims were not the first "to own the land." The original inhabitants were the *Bainuk*, an ethnic group whose name in Pakao is also a pejorative synonym for "non-Muslim." The name is said to derive from the Mandinko *bai*, "to chase away," implying that the Bainuk were driven off by Mandinka immigrants. Today, the Bainuk live in isolated settlements among the more populous Mandinko, Jola, and Balant people, west and south of Pakao.

Muslim ideology provides an explanation for the absence of any pre-Mandinka mythology, or indeed of very much early Mandinka mythology other than that concerned with the founding of villages. Such history is associated with infidel peoples. The few Bainuk kings remembered by name are those defeated or killed by Muslims in the nineteenth century *jihad*, and in these cases Bainuk is probably used to mean "non-Muslim," not the ethnic group. Islam was very likely a powerful force in determining which legends were passed on through succeeding generations. The term *Bainuk* itself is cleverly used by Mandinko to convey the impression that the early non-Muslims in Pakao were of a different ethnic group. Privately, some Mandinko admit that their own patrilineal ancestors were Mandinka infidels. There is a further reason for covering up the religious nature of one's origin, especially if it was fairly recently non-Muslim. In Mandinko, terms for non-Muslim easily invoke the image of slavery. Many non-Muslims captured in the *jihad* were enslaved; permanently relegating their descendants to the slave caste unless they could purchase freedom. The Mandinko use their preoccupation with origins to trace, if necessary mythically, a descent from Muslim forefathers. The discussion of origins is risky business because it can also validate some non-Muslim ancestry with all its impure connotations. The phrase "Pakao is eternal" is thus one way of avoiding the difficult and controversial question of ancestry.

To learn the homeland of the original Pakao immigrants, I collected the founding myth for each village. Of the twenty-four Pakao villages listed by Bertrand-Bocandé (1849:60–61), seventeen still exist, and the inhabitants of an eighteenth, Kounkali, now live in Dar Silamé. Seven of the villages trace their origin directly to Manding, the ancient Mali Empire. Four villages trace descent from Mandinka kingdoms along the Gambia River, Jarra, Badibu, Niani, and Wuli. Three villages claim descent from the kingdom of Kabu, southeast of Pakao. Two villages originated from Karantaba, the religious center on the south bank of the Casamance. One village is linked to the Wolof kingdom of Sine Saloum in the north of Senegal. The pattern of origins conforms with the list of kingdoms that successively dominated the area in previous centuries—namely, the Mali Empire, Kabu, and the Gambian kingdoms. The large number of villages linked to Manding suggests a correlation between the first Pakao villages and the expansionist era of the Mali Empire in the thirteenth and fourteenth centuries.

In Pakao myths about the founding of villages, the hero is guided in his selection of a site by divine inspiration. Another common feature of the myths is the reference to a sacred tree associated with the village founder. These trees, still respected by the present villagers, are believed to harbor demon-spirits protective of the founder's village. In Dar Silamé the founder's tree is a large *lenko*.[1] The myth recounts how Karimou Siaka Dramé, a hunter from Karantaba, slept under the tree when he dreamed of building a village nearby. In Mankono Ba the founder, Mama Toumane Sagnan, cured his male slave of snakebite with bark from the *katirao* tree.[2] Villagers in Mankono claim that the modern *katirao* sprouted from the root of the original. The location of the tree is a secret kept from other villagers. Mankoto Ba Camera, the founder of Soumboundou, was buried near the large *sito* tree[3] that he planted. The village of Karantaba takes its name from the *tabo* tree[4] where the founder, Fodé Heraba Dramé, read the Koran with his followers. The founding myths are, in short, a good illustration of the Mandinka tendency to perceive historical events in terms of heroes.

EARLY ISLAM

Islam in the lower Senegambia was an evolutionary force prior to the *jihads* of the mid-nineteenth century. Our knowledge of this period of Islamization is derived in large measure from the journals of explorers and traders who visited the area from the fifteenth through the nineteenth centuries. One of the more detailed early accounts of the Mandinko was provided by the Englishman Richard Jobson. His trading vessel reached the Gambia River in November 1620, and he plied the river for several months into the following year. Jobson was employed

---

[1] *Afzelia africana.*
[2] *Schrebera arborea.*
[3] *Adansonia digitata.*
[4] *Cola cordifolia.*

by the Company of Adventurers Trading to Guinea and Benin. This company was chartered in 1618 with the primary aim of locating the gold trade rumored to be flourishing in the Senegambia and elsewhere in West Africa. The commercial purpose of the venture is suggested by the title Jobson chose for his book, *The Golden Trade*. Although he found little gold, his contacts with villages along the Gambia produced a valuable description of the society of *marabouts* in the early seventeenth century. Two principal duties of a *marabout* were to instruct his male children in the Koran and to provide medicinal charms to non-Muslims. These earlier *marabouts* also provided medicinal charms to non-Muslim kings (Jobson 1968:85–86 and 63–64). In Jobson's time Mandinka society was composed of Muslims and non-Muslims and was less integrated than the Islamized society of today. Despite services performed for non-Muslims, the *marabouts* maintained their social distinctiveness with caste-like rigidity. They lived in separate villages and married only the daughters of *marabouts*. The sole non-Muslims permitted to live in their villages were slaves. Slaves married within their own caste and remained, in Jobson's words, "perpetuall bondsmen." Non-Muslim freemen lived in their own villages (Jobson 1968:78–79).

Jobson describes the *marabouts* as a religiously activist group, carving out and maintaining a place in society. Certainly Islam had made a powerful impact by this time, and in fact had been reported nearly two centuries earlier by the first Portuguese navigators to reach the Gambia River. In 1456, Fernandes recorded that "much of the country follow the Muslim religion," and he noted the presence of "many . . . priests [*marabouts*] going about the country teaching the faith to the people" (1951:45).

Despite centuries of contact with non-Muslims, the Muslim population of the Senegambia continued to live separately until roughly the mid-nineteenth century. Throughout this period, the *marabouts* never seem to have had much political power; yet they had a bizarre hold over those non-Muslims who purchased their charms. Jobson noticed this as well. In the eighteenth century, Moore (1738: 39–40) and Park (1969:28) were similarly impressed by the belief of non-Muslims in charms written by *marabouts*. Moore (1738:39–40) suggests that *marabouts* profited from the sale of these charms, which they sold at "a great price" to non-Muslims. He concluded that the early eighteenth-century "*marabouts* are generally richer and have a greater plenty of things about them."

The journals of Mungo Park, a Scottish explorer credited with discovering the Niger River, offer further insight into the process of Islamization.[5] Park thought of Islam as a civilizing force in a society dominated by non-Muslims. Although the Muslims formed a minority, they were evangelical and Park observed that Islam was making "considerable progress" (1969:11). Park's observations of

---

[5] Mungo Park arrived in the Gambia in 1795, at the age of twenty-four. Eventually, he learned to speak Mandinko fluently. He took relatively little European equipment with him, and relied on local acquaintances and food for sustenance. He returned to England in 1797, and his journal, published in 1799, became a best-seller in London. Park's life ended in tragedy during his second visit to the Senegambia in 1805. This time the explorer made the mistake of leading a large expedition and setting off at the height of the rainy season. One by one, his men died of malaria and other causes. Park died when his raft was ambushed on the Niger River.

ritual life were at times meticulous, and show how easily the local Islamic faith accommodated nonbelievers. The infant's naming ceremony, for example, was conducted in "the same" way regardless of whether the child's parents were Muslim or non-Muslim (1969:206–207). The infant's head was shaved a week

Dar Silamé: The central moment of the infant's naming ceremony is when the baby's head is shaved. Here the midwife, Dodo Daffé, an elder of Cissé hamlet, holds the baby during the shaving.

after birth. A *marabout* led prayers during the ceremony and announced the child's name for the first time. A sheep or goat was slain if the parents were sufficiently well-off. To conclude the ceremony, balls of freshly pounded dough, blessed by the *marabout*, were distributed to the guests. The infant's naming ceremony of today is virtually identical to this one described by Park 180 years ago. Even the name of the ceremony is nearly the same: *kulio* today ("head shaving"), *ding koon lee* in Park's time ("the child's head shaving"). We know, then, that a ritual practiced by devout Muslims today, punctuated with several Islamic prayers, was carried out by both Muslims and non-Muslims in Park's time. It is tempting to explain the durability of the ceremony in terms of its compatibility with Muslims and non-Muslims alike. Park states that both participated in the ritual. Are we to believe that these cooperating non-Muslims do not accept Islam? Are we to believe that the non-Muslims who purchase charms from *marabouts* do not accept Islam? The line beween a believer and a nonbeliever is very fine; there may well have been many nominal believers. The Islam described by explorers of the seventeenth and eighteenth centuries is flexible and tolerant, and is also proselytizing. The charm medicines and the ability to lead a ritual such as the naming ceremony were effective means of penetrating non-Muslim life.

Unfortunately, some questions cannot be answered from the accounts provided by explorers. How did Muslims and non-Muslims tell each other apart? Was it simply a matter of who prayed five times daily and who did not? Perhaps some of those who prayed were non-Muslims, who neither believed in what they did nor were instructed in the Koran. Residence may have been one way of telling who belonged to which group, since it is widely reported that the separate-village system existed until the mid-nineteenth century *jihad*. The appeal of charm medicine and the leadership of *marabouts* in ritual life imply that Islam had a certain prestige for non-Muslims. What might have accounted for this prestige? One explanation is writing. The explorer Jobson (1968:85–86) gave significant attention to the ability of seventeenth-century *marabouts* to write Arabic script (on wooden tablets, by the way, that seem identical to ones used in Pakao today). The literary skills of the early *marabouts* were devoted in part to writing the charm medicines, and these obviously made an impression on the non-Muslims. To a contemporary Mandinko, written charms are still the most important medicine, and the Mandinka word for charm (*safo*) means "writing." Until they can write passages from the Koran in Arabic, Pakao students are not considered educated.

THE PAKAO *JIHAD* OF 1843

From the 1840s until 1901, the area between the Casamance and Gambia Rivers was almost continuously at war. The first successful *jihad* during this warfare era occurred in Pakao in 1843. Led by Syllaba and based in Dar Silamé, the *jihad* forces killed the non-Muslim king of Pakao and many of his followers at the battle of Manduari. The decisive victory was followed by other successes, allowing Muslim forces by 1850 to gain control of Pakao and the adjacent kingdoms in central Casamance; the exceptions were a few non-Muslim villages near the French fort at Sédhiou. Both Quinn (1972:67–68) and Leary (1969) point to the *jihad* of 1843 as a breakthrough in the militant advance of Islam in the area. Today, the legend of Syllaba is widely told in Pakao to explain the triumph of Islam. In a sense, it constitutes the origin myth for the country as a whole, in a unifying way that myths about the founding of individual villages cannot emulate.

It is not often that an anthropologist can analyze a mythological event in terms of accounts recorded by eyewitnesses. We are permitted such an evaluation of the Pakao *jihad* by explorers' accounts and by letters from the Sédhiou fort that are now located in the Senegalese National Archives.[6]

The sources point to three basic preconditions for the *jihad*. First, powerful

[6] There are some 120 letters for the years 1842–1844, as well as treaties and other documents and letters. In order to give a more uninterrupted presentation of the *jihad*, I have mentioned only the most important sources. They have been cited completely in my Ph.D. thesis in the Bodleian Library, Oxford, England.

Dar Silamé: Munko *bread is passed out to the boys of the Koranic school in Sylla hamlet. It is sunrise. Seated around a bonfire, the men and boys have kept a vigil all night to celebrate the twenty-sixth day of Ramadan. They sing religious songs and recite from the Koran. All Mandinka boys in Pakao learn to read and write Koran Arabic at these schools.*

Fula kingdoms east of Pakao were already engaged in a war against non-Muslims well before the 1840s. The kingdom of Futa Jalon was, in fact, an ally of Pakao during the 1843 *jihad.* The cooperation and proximity of this kingdom to the east gave the Pakao *jihad* a certain inevitability, in that it was one engagement in a much broader conflict. On his second journey through eastern Senegal in 1805, Mungo Park noted an increase in religious warfare, reporting that the king of Futa Jalon had conquered the non-Muslim village of Julifunda and forced its inhabitants to adopt Islam (1969:303). Thirteen years later, Mollien passed through the same area and recorded that the Fula kingdoms of Futa Toro, Bundu, and Futa Jalon "had formed a sacred alliance for exterminating idolatry and waging eternal war with the Pagans" (1967:149).

A second cause of the Pakao *jihad* was the concentration of Muslims already living in the kingdom. This observation is based on the report by Bertrand-Bocandé that just prior to the *jihad* of 1843 there were nineteen Muslim villages in Pakao compared with five non-Muslim ones (1849:60–61). We can do no more than guess what this meant in terms of relative population, although Bertrand-Bocandé himself states that population was a factor in the *jihad* and that Pakao Muslims had become "more numerous" (1849:57). Muslim villages also outnumbered non-Muslim villages in Suna and Balmadou, two kingdoms opposite Pakao on the south bank of the Casamance. The *jihad* succeeded in these two kingdoms, but not immediately in Boudié, where the fort at Sédhiou was located and where non-Muslim villages were in the majority (Bertrand-Bocandé 1848:60–62 and 334–335).

A third and final cause of the *jihad* has to do with economic destabilization brought about by the establishment of French trading posts in central Casamance. In 1837 a fort and commercial center were inaugurated at Sédhiou, in the kingdom of Boudié. By 1840 the French had located trading posts in the neighboring kingdoms of Pakao and Suna, near the villages of Soumboundou and Sandinièri. As a condition for establishing these outposts, the French signed treaties with the monarchs of the three kingdoms, providing them with an annual rent for the use of territory. The problem with this seemingly orderly arrangement was that it provided income to non-Muslim kings and largely ignored the Muslims who lived in a majority of the villages in both Pakao and Suna. Evidently, the French chose to negotiate and sign the treaties with titular kings whose authority may have been quite nominal over the Muslims. The non-Muslim king of Boudié, with whom the French signed the first treaty, was described by the Sédhiou commander as a drunken, pathetic figurehead, dependent on the French for income, liquor, and consumer goods. Briefly, the system established by the French stressed economic relationships with non-Muslims, providing them with a wealth disproportionate to their ability to rule.

There were signs of impending warfare in the early months of 1843. An army from Futa Jalon, estimated to be between 7000 and 8000, entered the vicinity. After a relative lull, one of the first attacks was made by Karantaba against the village of Manduari on the night of March 28. By April 9, fighting had erupted in several areas, and the French, protectively sequestered in the Sédhiou fort, observed that the Muslim forces had taken over the country by revolutionary force. Despite the initial decisiveness of the French reports, Muslims and non-Muslims continued to raid each other. On May 1 in a bold dawn attack, Pakao Muslim forces killed the king of Bakoum and made off with some ninety captives, mostly women and children. The fighting brought trade to a halt, greatly disturbing the French, who had established a presence initially for commercial reasons. The Fula army, led by a warrior named Bakary Koing, roamed independantly of the Pakao Muslims. In November Koing negotiated directly with the French in an attempt to collect taxes from both Boudié kingdom and Soumboundou in the kingdom of Pakao. The French refused to deal, and Koing stubbornly blockaded the fort for a week. Suddenly, Koing and his army were summoned to Dar Silamé to attend a council of chiefs from the kingdoms of Pakao, Balmadou, and Suna, to consider the Fula request for taxes. On November 26, Koing reportedly fell from his horse in Dar Silamé and died, putting an end to his scheme for exacting tribute. The French then learned that Koing had played a supporting rather than the leading role, as they once thought. Prior to the outbreak of fighting, Koing had been summoned to Pakao by an influential *marabout* named Sylla for the purpose of fighting non-Muslims.

With the arrival of the new year, 1844, economic factors behind the warfare were increasingly evident in the French reporting. The commanding officer of the garrison negotiated compensation from the Muslims for goods they had pillaged from the trading posts. Evidently the Muslims had not completely subordinated economic motives to religious ones. As the warfare spread to neighboring kingdoms, reports circulated of non-Muslim armies fighting each other. Sylla led his Muslim forces against villagers from Mankono, presumably Muslim, in order to recoup rent paid them the previous year. From January through March the fighting intensified, and a Pakao/Fula army threatened to attack the Sédhiou fort unless the French made rental payments withheld during the fighting. The commanding officer at Sédhiou learned that the traders were reaping profits by supplying the Muslims, and he ordered them to cease commercial operations.

By the end of May, villages along both banks of the Casamance River were involved in the fighting. A Muslim force approached the fort, intending to storm it, but a thundershower prevented the operation from being carried out. In July, the envoys of Sylla returned to Sédhiou village outside the fort and paid off its chief to convert to Islam and to stop harboring Muslims. In the Muslim view, the French were passive allies of the non-Muslims. During September, representatives of the Fula army convinced the inexperienced French commander to sign a neutrality treaty whereby non-Muslims would be refused refuge in the fort. The treaty was later disavowed by the French.

The economic content of the *jihad* was perhaps best revealed in a Pakao raid against the docks of the Sédhiou fort on September 22. Led by Sylla, the raiders took twelve stevedores prisoner and made off with merchandise from the warehouse. Four of the prisoners later escaped and reported more than 6000 Pakao and Fula troops gathered at Dar Silamé. Outraged at this harassment of trade, the French commander, a lieutenant named Caternault, declared war on Pakao and requested a heavily armed column of 400 men from the colonial capital on the island of Gorée. The French failed in their attempts to negotiate directly with Sylla. He sent a message stating that he would make peace only if Caternault himself visited Dar Silamé and agreed to pay 1100 gourds worth of tribute to the Muslims (said to be 250 francs at the time). The treaty establishing a trading post in Pakao obligated the French to pay a rent of only 50 gourds annually. While Caternault waited for the column from Gorée, he learned the cause of the raid. The Muslims were outraged that a trader posted in Soumboundou refused credit to a chief until his debts were paid. Caternault accused the traders of profiteering and ordered them to sign a statement binding them not to supply Muslims with weapons.

Relations remained tense. The Muslims warily awaited the attack threatened by the French. A council of important Pakao chiefs met in October and, it is reported, severely reprimanded Sylla. They sent a delegation to the fort to sue for peace. The delegation agreed to make Sylla pay the French an indemnity of 250 gourds; as a sign of good faith they left behind the Mankono chief's son as a hostage. In November, a single envoy from Gorée arrived in Sédhiou by riverboat, rebuked Caternault for his threat of war, and temporarily relieved him of command. As the year drew to a close, the frustrated envoy proposed a scheme to secure the indemnity from Sylla. He would deduct the value of the stolen merchandise from the rent the French owed to Pakao. Unfortunately, the Sédhiou dispatches are incomplete for the years 1845–1851, and we do not know how

Sylla fares. Several treaties signed during this time period indicate a winding down of the *jihad*. In 1851, Boudié was the first kingdom to become a French protectorate. Hecquard reports that the few non-Muslims remaining in Pakao, Suna, and Balmadou were politically disorganized and were prevented by the dominant Muslims from fortifying the village areas left to them (1855:123).

As told today, the Pakao legend of the *jihad* is markedly different. The legend makes no mention of the economic factors that dominate French reporting, except briefly to accuse the non-Muslims of having pillaged Muslim villages prior to the *jihad* (the reports for 1842 do not record this). Instead, the legend focuses on exploits of the *marabout* Syllaba, whose fame is indicated by the suffix *ba* ("great") attached to his name. I recorded several versions of the legend in villages of Pakao and neighboring Suna, but the best was told by chief Fodé Ibrahima Dramé of Dar Silamé. His version is summarized as follows.

"The father of Syllaba came from the east." The legend begins typically with a reference to the east, setting a religious tone readily understood by Pakao Muslims. Syllaba's father lived first in Ouducari, then in Dar Silamé, where he married the daughter of a great *marabout* named Cissé. He later returned to Ouducari. Syllaba was born there and distinguished himself as a youth in Koranic school. While still a young man, Syllaba traveled to Karamba Touba in Futa Jalon to continue his religious studies. He came back to Ouducari as a *marabout* and instructed his students in the Koran. This was during the time of Nyedumasani, a cruel infidel king of Manduari, whose followers persisted in raiding Muslim villages. One Friday after mosque, Syllaba proposed to the elders of Ouducari that he launch a holy war against Nyedumasani. At Syllaba's insistence, the debate continued at mosque for several Fridays, until the elders would have no more of it. Fearful of Nyedumasani's wrath, they drove Syllaba from the mosque, beat him, and burned his religious books.

Infuriated and dejected, Syllaba sought help from the Cissé of Dar Silamé, his mother's brothers. They sympathized with his scheme to attack Manduari but would not commit themselves until Dramé, the chiefly hamlet, also agreed. The Dramé consented on the condition that an alliance could be formed with Karantaba, the religious center and ancestral Dramé home. Karantaba went along with the plan, but the cautious Syllaba sought an ally in another direction. He sent a messenger requesting troops to Alemamy, the King of Futa Jalon. The non-Muslims knew about Sylla's lengthy preparations, and they laughed at him. Jokingly, they labeled as a "Muslim messenger" any child who took too long doing an errand. The Alemamy of Futa eventually sent Bakary Koing and a small contingent of warriors to aid the Pakao Muslims. The warriors of Karantaba, Dar Silamé, and other Pakao villages joined forces, but all was not quite ready. Depending on the version, either Syllaba or a great *marabout* from Karantaba announced that he possessed a secret weapon, holy water (that is, a water charm). Syllaba asked for a volunteer and instructed him to put on the ragged clothes of a madman. Thus disguised, he was told to enter Manduari and pour the holy water into the wells, into household water jars, and in a circle around the village. The gourd carrying the holy water was to be pierced so that water could trickle out. The volunteer completed the mission and returned safely to Dar Silamé. At this point, one version claims that a flaming star fell on Manduari and destroyed it. The chief's version, which is more prevalent, says that a unified Pakao force launched a furious dawn assault against Manduari, killing the king and many other infidels. Syllaba ordered his forces to present captured warriors with a grim choice, death or Islam. Several non-Muslim women hung themselves in the wells of Manduari, preferring death to enslavement by a *marabout*. The Muslim triumph ended with a speech by Syllaba to the faithful, elaborating the ideals of the *jihad*. He declared that the war was made for the religious purpose of vanquishing infidels. He asked the faithful to continue the spreading of Islam. Finally, Syllaba renounced not only material gain from the *jihad*, but the idea that he or any of his sons would ever become a king of Pakao.

A striking feature of the legend is its careful construction of a system of alliances, bringing Pakao together as a religious polity. Following the setback in Ouducari, which suggests Muslim weakness, Syllaba is linked successively with his mother's brothers, the Dramé, Karantaba, the kingdom of Futa Jalon, and other Pakao villages. The chief's version is careful to "make" Syllaba show his deference to the Dramé of both Dar Silamé and Karantaba. The alliance and a successful mission are ultimately blessed and brought about by the grace of Allah, as demonstrated in the myth by the miraculous power of the holy water (a water charm). It is possible that the water is not merely a mythical idiom for divine cooperation. One report by a contemporary French observer describes the role of holy water in Muslim battle preparations. The report is by Hecquard, the French explorer who in 1851 lived for three months on the south bank of the Casamance River. He witnessed first-hand the piety and strength of belief with which Muslims carried out raids against non-Muslims (1855:99–100): Bakary Koye (not Bakary Koing) assembled his warriors under a large tree and distributed weapons. "This task complete, a *marabout* brought before him a gourd full of water, into which he put salt, millet and a bit of bread. Then rising, he prayed aloud for the success of the mission, with all those present reciting after him. Next he blesses the water and all those who take part in the expedition, with each man in his turn approaching him, taking water in his hands, splashing his face and arms while murmuring a prayer. . . . These men are firmly convinced that this water preserves true believers against all dangers and that those killed, who have touched the water, go straight to paradise, especially when they die fighting infidels."

If the French accounts serve as a guide, the incidents after the battle of Manduari have been edited out of the legend by mythical authors. On the one hand, it seems fair enough to suggest that Islamic and social values shaped this mythical editing process. On the other hand, the French may have been biased toward economic factors because of their own commercial interests. They may have misunderstood the charismatic nature of Syllaba's role and the importance of the first Muslim victory at Manduari. Was Syllaba finally as controversial among his people as implied by French reports? Did Muslim orthodoxy require that he be recast in myths as a saint? Was he the greedy war lord portrayed by the French, or was he merely defending the legitimate interests of his people? Influenced by Islam, did the post-*jihad* concept of Pakao require a legend validating the decentralized religious confederation by equating political purity with the absence of kingship?

If there was one area of Mandinka life changed and even devastated by the *jihad*, it was in the field of politics. We know from Bertrand-Bocandé that a system of rotating kingship existed before the *jihad*. The chiefs of the royal capital villages successively became king, in circulating fashion, without having to change residence. In Pakao there were four such alternating capitals, with Manduari serving as the king's residence at the time of the *jihad* (1849:60–61). After the *jihad* the rotating system vanished, and there is no further mention of Manduari in sources.

THE WARFARE ERA

In the 1840s, while Pakao was winning and solidifying its *jihad*, there were outbreaks of fighting in the kingdoms of Jimara and Combo along the Gambia River (Quinn 1972:67–69). In Combo in the 1850s the Muslim forces gained a dominant position vis-á-vis the non-Muslims, bringing open confrontation with the British. In the 1860s, a *marabout* named Maba Diakhou organized a war which had an enormous impact in the kingdoms along the Gambia. Although others prepared the way with scattered revolts, Maba escalated the *jihad* into a force that, even after he died, succeeded in toppling the remaining non-Muslim kingdoms, accelerating the Islamization of the Gambian basin. Maba began his *jihad* in the kingdom of Badibu, and fighting quickly spread to neighboring kingdoms as other non-Muslim groups gained confidence. In 1862 Maba was defeated at a large battle against the non-Muslims and their French allies outside the French fort in Kaolak. In 1863 he was badly beaten by non-Muslims at the town of Kwinella in Kiang. Despite these setbacks, the *jihad* was pressed forward along the Gambia by other Muslim leaders. Maba's own territorial initiatives were then concentrated in the north of Senegal, and he fought several battles with the French. Finally in 1867, after his army had been harassed by a French force, Maba was slain in a battle against the non-Muslim Serer in the Sine region north of Gambia.[7]

Other leaders rose to succeed Maba, beginning with his younger brother Mamur and including his son later on. To Mandinko south of the Gambia, the most important of the late nineteenth-century *jihad* leaders was Fodé Kaba.[8] Legends of his exploits are now widely told between the Casamance and Gambia Rivers, where most of his battles and raids took place. During his long career, Fodé Kaba fought on several fronts, beginning, curiously enough, against a neighboring Muslim people. In 1862 he started a blood feud with Alfa Molo, the leader of the Fula people east of Pakao, after Molo killed his father and destroyed his town. The feud continued after Alfa was succeeded by his son Moussa Molo, and about 1876 reached a high point at the battle of Kerewan in eastern Pakao. Both armies are said to have lost so many men that neither side could claim victory. The battle

---

[7] For an account of Maba and a good history of the Senegambia, see Charlotte Quinn (1972). For an additional perspective on Maba, see Leary (1969).

[8] For the career of Fodé Kaba, see Quinn (1972:170–174), Leary (1969), and Roche (1970 and 1971).

is still considered controversial because Muslims are not supposed to fight each other. From the 1860s through the turn of the century, Kaba's cavalry also raided non-Muslim Jola, Mandinka, and other peoples. His army lived off the spoils of war, sold many captives into slavery, and never stayed in one place long enough to establish a capital.

Fodé Kaba is probably best remembered for his resistance against the French. This is due mostly to the battle of Mandina, where he was killed. In 1901 the French had tired of Kaba's persistent militance and decided to send an expeditionary force against him. In March, the French column caught up with him at Mandina, a village northeast of Pakao and south of the Gambia. Determined to hold out, Kaba and his army took up positions in a Mandinka fort. Their women and children were also inside. Backed by artillery, the French leveled the fort and killed Kaba along with many of his followers. The Mandinka version of his death was recounted to me by Fodé Ibrahima Dramé. Fodé Kaba had foreseen that he would die at the hands of the French. In Mandina he ordered his men to dig a tomb inside the walls of his fort. As the moment of attack drew near, he knelt on his prayer-mat with beads in hand and was killed by a rifle shot in the forehead. He was quickly buried. When the fort was blasted to ruins, the walls covered up the grave. The French looked in vain for Kaba's body as proof of his death. As a war trophy they cut off the head of another slain elder who resembled him.

If we think of it in time and on a geopolitical scale, the warfare era occurred as two historical trends converged. From the west came the colonials who gradually converted their interest in trade to a quest for territory. From the east came Muslims in increasing numbers and finally in a series of dramatic revolutionizing *jihads* in the nineteenth century. In the Casamance and along the Gambia River, the *marabout* leaders of the most important *jihads* had a common characteristic that merits attention. Syllaba, Maba Diakhou, and Fodé Kaba were all considered "outsiders" by the old, established Mandinka lineages who, in many cases, traced ancestry to Manding. To Mandinko, the concept of "stranger" or "outsider" (*luntao*) is an enduring status, one that implies both limited acceptance and the potential for controversy. Maba was of Torodo (Fula) and Wolof descent and was the son of a *marabout* from Futa Toro. The Wolof ancestry in particular was distasteful to some Mandinko, who thought it was wrong for a stranger to lead a *jihad* (Quinn 1972:129). Fodé Kaba was of Jakhanke ancestry and, like Maba, was the son of a *marabout* with roots in eastern Senegal. Syllaba was also the son of a Jakhanke *marabout*, said to have immigrated to Pakao from the village of Bani Israile in Bundu, eastern Senegal. The three *jihad* leaders had paternal ties to a more orthodox and proselytizing Islamic tradition to the east. The Jakhanke in particular have a proselytizing role that is centuries old. In a study of the Jakhanke, Smith concludes that they consider themselves among "the oldest and most religious of black Muslims and speak of their role as *marabouts* as their reason for being" (1965:235). It was an aggressive and fundamentalist Islam that the *jihad* leaders preached to the more traditional Mandinka Muslims who received them.

5/Social action

MARRIAGE

Mandinka marriage does not happen on one day or even over a period of several years. It is a process occurring throughout the lifetime of individuals, accompanied by required gifts. The marriage system often begins with infant betrothal and near the end of life permits a form of old-age marriage.

Many girls are betrothed within hours of their birth. The "father's sister" places a cord around the baby's wrist and claims her as a future wife for her son. Infant betrothal is an old practice among the Mandinko and was described by Francis Moore in the 1730s (1738:131). This arrangement was binding, and the girl could not marry someone else unless given permission by her betrothed. Today, the betrothed youth is not always consulted when the girl seeks another partner. However, the two families can make it most difficult for the girl to break off the betrothal. The role of the father's sister does not stop after she makes her claim. To confirm the betrothal, she presents small gifts of cloth and rice to the infant girl's mother. The future husband, often a boy less than twelve years old, has no income of his own to do this. He takes over from his mother as soon as he is able and relinquishes his betrothal option if he ever stops. One effect of the betrothal system is to make it more difficult for young men without a betrothed to find a wife. Another effect is to facilitate matrilateral cross-cousin marriage, since betrothal occurs only when a man's sister claims his infant daughter for her son.

A suitor enters a contract for a wife when he makes the first bride-price payment to her parents. The first installment of about 10,000 CFA, called "wife-searching money," is divided equally between the girl's mother and father. Five kola nuts and a kilo of salt are also given by the prospective husband "to show his respect." From this point the marriage has taken place. The girl sleeps with her husband, in his house, on an intermittent basis. She continues, however, to spend most of her nights in her father's household, where she prepares her husband's food and washes his clothes. She remains in her father's household in an economic sense, since she is in effect a member of his work force.

The second and final bride price payment, called "confirmation money," is usually presented within a year after the first installment. The second payment tends to be made during the months of January, February, or March, after the harvest is sold, providing the husband with the necessary cash.

The case of Suntukun Demba is typical. In January of 1974 he gave Keba Dramé 8200 CFA and three kilos of kola nuts (costing 1425 CFA), to complete the bride price for Keba's daughter Mabintu. The total bride price, including the first installment, came to 19,625 CFA. Suntukun presented the second payment to Keba at a meeting of his subhamlet. The men said prayers and passed around kola nuts. The money was then distributed, with greater amounts going to the older men in relation to their age and relative generations. Five hundred CFA was saved out of the total to buy a prayer mat each for the five eldest men of the wife-giving hamlet, Dramé. Some kola nuts were also set aside for them. The head of the wife-giving hamlet, the village chief Fodé Ibrahima, convened a marriage confirmation meeting attended by the men of his hamlet. The men again said prayers for the couple and for their future offspring. Kola nuts were distributed. As a final order of business the men decided on how much "bride gift" to require of the husband. The bride gift is either one heifer, two sheep, or two goats. The hamlet elders usually ask for two goats, at 1000 CFA each the least expensive sum. The goats are given to the wife on the same day she is permanently transferred from her father's people to the husband's hamlet, and they remain her property. If the bride gift is not paid, then the wife-taking hamlet is not able to claim full ownership of the couple's offspring in the event of divorce.

After some three to seven years, a husband formally asks his parents-in-law to allow their daughter to be transferred permanently to his household. At the time of the request he gives his mother-in-law a goat, a skirt, a prayer mat, and a leather Koran cover which she gives to her brother. The cost of these "mother's gifts" totals 1700 CFA. The actual transfer of the bride still does not take place for another two years.

If the process of obtaining a wife seems long and expensive, a prospective Mandinka husband would not disagree. His wife's family postpones the date of transfer for as long as possible. Husbands consider their fathers-in-law to be "difficult men." The required gifts and payments and the length of the waiting period emphasize that the status of the husband and his people is lower than that of his wife's people.

By late 1974, the bride price was 25,000 CFA if the girl was from the husband's village. A girl from another village required 40,000 CFA. These figures had inflated dramatically compared with the totals of 15,000 CFA and 25,000 CFA asked for local and nonlocal girls in 1973. In 1974, the farmer's average income was only 20–25,000 CFA for the year.

The historical sources offer an interesting commentary on qualitative changes in bride price over the centuries. Beginning in the early seventeenth century, the nature of bride price evolved from goods to slaves, and finally in the twentieth century to cash, paralleling economic and social conditions of successive eras. In 1620–1621 Richard Jobson reported bride price as a feature of Mandinka marital negotiations. He observed that a bride was purchased for "some commoditie," without specifying the goods (1968:67). In the 1730s, Moore wrote that the bride price was two cows, two iron bars, and 200 kola nuts (1738:132). By the late eighteenth century, the imprint of the slave trade was greater; reflecting this trend, a typical bride price was two slaves, unless the attractiveness of the girl merited a higher number (Park 1969:204). As late as the mid-nineteenth century, Hecquard reported that slavery was the basis of bride price among Mandinka and Fula peoples in the vicinity of Pakao. The price was ten slaves for a freeborn woman and two for a slave (1855:20).

The marriage transaction does not cease once the various payments have been made and the day of transfer finally arrives. The modern ritual of bride transfer is elaborate for nobles and requires more attention than the comparatively simple ceremony for artisans, praise-singers, and slaves. Among nobles, the transfer takes place in the rainy season, a time of fertility coinciding with late July and early August when the crops begin to germinate. The appointed day is often a Thursday or Friday, the two holiest days of the week. The bride dresses in prescribed fashion, wearing a dark blue skirt, a white smock over her upper body, and a blue turban. As a veil, she drapes a dark blue shawl over her head and pulls it down to just above eye-level. She adorns herself with anklets and bracelets made of beads or silver. For good luck, she ties a silver coin to a front-piece of hair.

In Dar Silamé during the summer of 1974, a typical bride transfer took place as follows. The bride, Binta Dramé, waited in the house of her father, Fodé Kemo Dramé. Dressed ceremonially in a white smock and dark blue robe, the village queen, Koto Fadera, entered the house. For a small fee, she joyously performed a bride's dance. Koto then led Binta from her father's house to the house of her husband, Modi Samaté. The bride walked behind Koto, placing her hands on the queen's hips. Mandinko call this "carrying the bride," using the same verb when a mother "carries" an infant on her back. "Carrying the bride" has a symbolic importance, emphasizing the dominant role that the queen, leader of women's affairs in the village, will play in the bride's life. Linked together, Koto and Binta were followed by a throng of men, women, and children singing praise songs. They were met at the door of Modi Samaté's house by his best man. Binta went inside and sat on Modi's bed. Koto and the best man dropped the opaque mosquito net around her. Koto performed a second bridal dance in the house. Modi, who was waiting outside, greeted the queen as she left and paid her 1000 CFA. Modi went to the bed, lifted up the mosquito net and chatted with Binta.

This was the beginning of the seclusion period, lasting from the afternoon of transfer (first day) until the exit of the bride on the morning of the fourth day. The ritual is the same for any noble bride in Pakao. During seclusion, Binta never left Modi's house in the daytime. She did not see or talk to anyone except her husband. If she had to leave the house, she waited until late at night when everyone else was asleep. Modi went along to protect her from cannibal-witches. Food was brought to Binta during regular daylight hours. She received it from inside the mosquito netting without being seen. During most of the second and third days, Binta sat on the bed hidden from view. Kinswomen sat in the room with her, reporting village news and announcing her visitors. Even when greeted, Binta kept her silence.

The ritual of seclusion temporarily enforces and symbolizes the bride's devotion to her husband. It also stresses relationships with kinswomen. Seclusion protects

Dar Silamé: Koto Fadera, the village queen, escorts Binta Dramé from her father's people to her husband's. Both women wear the appropriate robes.

the bride from the cannibal-witch by shielding her from its sight. In Mandinka thought, people are most vulnerable to this evil spirit during transition periods, including circumcision and burial. The white burial shroud, the circumcision novice's costume, and the opaque mosquito net are all considered protective devices against the cannibal-witch.

The husband plays only a limited ritual role during seclusion and makes primarily an economic contribution to the festivities. Modi Samaté worked in the fields as usual. On the first two nights of seclusion, he paid for a feast held for his wife's people by his own hamlet. He also gave Binta a new set of work clothes, emphasizing that she was now fully within his work force.

On the morning of the fourth day, Binta left Modi's house. Her period of seclusion ceremonially ended when Koto unveiled her, removing a white cloth placed over her eyes. The women of the village stowed wedding gifts of cooking utensils in Modi's house, and then held a dance outside. After the dance, Binta ceremonially asked her husband's older brother for money and curtsied to him. This request acknowledged her new economic dependence on her husband's people. The first day after exiting from seclusion, Binta prepared a feast for Modi's (wife-taking) hamlet. This action demonstrated her gratitude and again stressed a change in economic relationships. The bridal period ended informally in November with the completion of the harvest, when brides ceased to wear any part of their costumes.

The ritual of bride transfer is the same when the noble woman happens to come from another village. However, slaves and artisan–praise-singers have neither a four-day seclusion nor a bridal costume. For them, the ritual of transfer may occur at any time of the year. The bride is escorted by the women to her husband's home. Sometimes these escorting women hold a dance in the evening. The bride exits from her husband's house the next morning. The women present her with gifts and hold another dance.

If we think of the ritual transfer, seclusion, and veiling of a bride as principles of action, then these notions have existed for a long time, even though the present elaborations differ as to style. In 1620–1621 Jobson described a transfer ceremony in which the husband and his friends forcibly abducted the bride. After a mock battle with her people, they carried her to the husband's dwelling, where she was secluded for an unspecified length of time. After seclusion she veiled her face for several months (1968:70–71). In the eighteenth century, both Francis Moore (1738:132) and Mungo Park (1969:204–205) were impressed by the veiling and ritual transfer of a bride, but neither explorer reported seclusion in the husband's house. Moore wrote that the veiled bride was brought on a man's shoulders from her parents' to her husband's house. Park recorded that the women escorted the bride to her husband's house and that her white bridal costume was designed to conceal her entire body.

There are several additional concepts related to marriage and children. The infant's naming ceremony is successively less elaborate for each of three child-bearing situations: (1) the birth of a woman's first child; (2) the birth of additional children prior to bride transfer; and (3) the birth of children after transfer. In cases where children are orphaned, they are invariably adopted, often by the husband's patrilineal kinsmen. The adopted child is expected to contribute exclusively to the work force of the foster parents. However, an adopted child always retains the patronym given at birth and does not take on the name of the foster parents. A preferred form of adoption is for a youth to live with his mother's brother. The adopted son benefits from this arrangement by marrying his mother's brother's daughter. He has the added advantage of marrying her for a low bride price (and in former times, it is said, for no bride price at all).

The Mandinko permit divorce and allow both men and women to remarry. Widows can be inherited, usually by the genealogical brother of the deceased husband. In most cases of remarriage, the widow or divorcée commands a lower bride price. Also, a noble woman goes through the ceremony of bride transfer and four-day seclusion but once. In cases of remarriage there is no ceremonial transfer.

Like many peoples, the Mandinko have prohibitions against incest and adultery. Adulterers are beaten or fined, although in some cases they are not punished except for the stigma society attaches to them. The punishment for adultery in previous centuries was more drastic, ranging from enslavement (Jobson 1968:67; Moore 1738:42 and 133; and Park 1969:227) to execution if the adulterer were a slave or poor person and the partner of higher rank (Hecquard 1855:120).

The Mandinko practice polygamy. Islam places numerical limits on the system of polygamy, constraining a man to a maximum of four wives at any one time. Jobson reported in the 1620s that a king was permitted seven wives along with official concubines (1968:65), and Moore (1738:133) stated that some men had 100 wives. In the late eighteenth century, Park observed that Muslims were restricted to four wives, implying that non-Muslims were allowed more (1969:205). Islam has also influenced the institution of old-age marriage. The Mandinko permit an older widow to name an elder man or grandson as a fictitious husband in order to comply with Muslim rules requiring that she be married at death.

ALLIANCE AND OPPOSITION

In Pakao villages, there are two sorts of alliances among hamlets. As mentioned in the second chapter, the one is a *sanao* alliance based on marriages between hamlets. The other is based on a bifurcated division of the village into "upper" and "lower." The hamlets lying in either division tend to be allies.

In Dar Silamé, the important hamlet alliance is between Cissé and Sylla, the two *sanao* hamlets that constitute upper village. Conflicts between Sylla and their rivals, the chiefly Dramé, force Cissé to take sides with Sylla. In the third chapter I described the fight between Dramé and Sylla over succession to the position of *imam*. Arfan Sanji pressed the candidacy of Sancoun by threatening the secession of Cissé and Sylla hamlets. This never actually happened, but Sancoun did found another village nearby. Fodé Ibrahima Dramé described another conflict illustrating the principles of opposition between Sylla and Dramé, and the alliance between Sylla and Cissé. The chief witnessed the incident as a boy. On a routine visit to Dar Silamé around the turn of the century, French soldiers picked oranges from a tree owned by Fodali Sylla. Not far from the *imam*'s house, they were challenged by Fodali's son Karamo. The brash young man scolded the French for picking oranges without permission, and they beat him. Realizing they had created an incident, the French ran to chief Lambanja Dramé for protection. Fodali was infuriated. He called on the riflemen of Sylla and Cissé to attack both the French and the Dramé. Lambanja sent a messenger saying he would fight Sylla and Cissé if he had to, and his personal intervention prevented a shoot-out just as the two sides formed battle lines in the center of the village. Fodé Ibrahima went on to explain that the gratitude of the French later saved Dar Silamé from destruction. A French column marched on the village following the battle of Mandina in 1901. The commander recognized Lambanja as the chief who had intervened with Fodali Sylla during the previous visit. Rather than burn Dar Silamé, the French confiscated arms and interrogated Fodali Sylla all day under the hot sun. According to Fodé Ibrahima Dramé, the French believed that Fodali was a king like Fodé Keba and was therefore dangerous to them. Fodali denied being a king and insisted to the French that he was merely a simple disciple of Islam. Lambanja's intervention not only saved the village, but may have saved Fodali's life.

Elsewhere in Pakao there are additional examples of serious opposition within villages. I found two villages where groups of hamlets seceded from each other without changing residence. In each case the village was reorganized politically to form new villages. In Marandao, two villages were recently established after a long dispute over a chieftainship that rotated between two hamlets descended from the village founders. In Diana Ba, the largest Pakao village, four new villages were established in place and a second mosque was built, following another recent dispute over succession to chieftainship. I did not stay long enough in these villages to determine the role of *sanao* relations and land divisions. In two other cases of village strife, the distinction between upper and lower village was fundamental.

Sometime in the early 1960s, a Baro man from upper village in Mankono Ba killed a species of duck that was the totem of Sagnan, the chiefly hamlet. The outraged Sagnan punished the man by preventing him from attending mosque. The hamlets in upper village where he lived (and where many Dramé *marabouts* and *imams* had lived) threatened to secede and build a new mosque, until the dispute was resolved some weeks later. Karantaba was the scene of another incident. In 1973, a brawl broke out between upper and lower village after a fire. The damage was concentrated in the more densely populated upper village, where most of the village chiefs and *imams* had lived. A local government official suggested ploughing a grid of roads through the village to minimize the destruction caused by any future fire. Upper village, largely demolished, accepted the plan since it had little to lose anyway. Lower village objected because some of its undamaged houses would be bulldozed down. The local government could not proceed with the proposal until fully backed by the entire village. The indecision kept upper village from rebuilding its houses. One disgruntled man from upper village started a fight with men from lower village during Friday prayers at mosque. The fighting spread through the village, and several men were arrested by the local authorities. The roads were later ploughed.

In Mankono Ba and Karantaba, the pattern of *sanao* relations does not seem to

Karantaba: A proud father displays the toy airplane that he carved for his son. The model was copied after the plane flying regularly over the village.

have contributed to the disputes. In both cases *sanao* relations join hamlet pairs across the division between upper and lower villages. In Dar Silamé the opposite is true, since the *sanao* pair of Sylla/Cissé lies entirely in upper village (and Dramé/Samaté is in lower). In general, *sanao* relations caused a relatively high number of marriages between each hamlet pair.[1] In terms of marriage, the *sanao* hamlets thus tended to be overintegrated with each other and underintegrated with the other hamlets in the village. This facilitated the political isolation of Cissé and Sylla from the rest of the village.

KINSHIP

"If you cut the beard, only dust falls off; but if you cut the breast, blood is spilled." This Pakao proverb illustrates the Mandinka view that the mother holds the dominant position in determining kinship. The maternal idiom is also reflected

---

[1] See Table 2 of the extant marriages in Dar Silamé. With some exceptions, statistical tests on the table confirm the idea in Dar Silamé that its *sanao* relations are linked to a high number of marriages between the paired hamlets. See Chapter 6 of my D.Phil. thesis.

TABLE 2   DAR SILAMÉ: EXTANT MARRIAGES OF LIVING MALES

Wife-Taking Hamlet	Wife-Giving Hamlet								
	Cissé	Dramé	Sylla	Samaté	Daffé	Gitté Dabo Demba	Sagnan	Females of Other Villages	Totals
Cissé	0	20	11	1	10	1	0	3	46
Dramé	24	0	6	27	18	4	0	10	89
Sylla	6	12	0	5	2	0	0	5	30
Samaté	2	23	3	0	9	6	0	1	44
Daffé	6	16	3	2	0	0	0	2	29
Gitté Dabo Demba	4	9	1	4	4	0	0	2	24
Immigrants Sagnan	0	0	0	0	0	0	0	2	2
Males in Other Villages	0	4	1	0	1	3	3	0	12
Totals	42	84	25	39	44	14	3	25	276

Marriages by immigrants before arriving in Dar Silamé are disregarded, unless they occurred with a Dar Silamé girl. In this case, they figure in the total for males in other villages.

in the preferential system of matrilateral cross-cousin marriage (descent is patrilineal). The rule of preference for a man is that "you marry your mother's brother's daughter." Older men state the preference this way: "You marry your daughter to your sister's son." There are negative rules saying that a man must not marry his father's sister's daughter or his parallel cousin. At least one elder *marabout*, Arfanba Sagnan, insisted that a man could ignore the rules and marry whomever he desired. Despite this view, three of his six total marriages were with matrilateral cross-cousins. Mandinka men in Pakao do in fact marry large numbers of these cousins. In Dar Silamé in late 1972, 126 out of 264 extant marriages (48 percent) were with matrilateral cross-cousins, both genealogical and classificatory.

The maternal emphasis is seen in the kinship terminology itself. *Ba*, the word for mother, is the root word in compound terms for mother's brother, mother's brother's daughter, sister, and brother.[2] All of these relatives are important in the system of matrilateral cross-cousin marriage. Another indication of the matrilateral preference occurs in certain equations within the kinship terminology. In the study of kinship, an equation is the denotation by the same word of two or more different relatives. Thus, from the male perspective, MB=WF, ZS=DH, and WM=MBW. Taking the first equation, for example, the word *baring* means both "mother's brother" and "wife's father" ("father-in-law"). When a girl marries, her father linguistically becomes a "mother's brother" to the new husband, even if there were no prior kinship. In the preferential system, the wife's father might already be the mother's brother of her husband, but otherwise the marriage converts

[2] In Mandinko these are *baring, baringdingo, baringmuso,* and *baringke.*

the wife's father to the same kinship term for mother's brother. Such an equation is quasi-prescriptive, for in every marriage it can give the appearance that a man has married the daughter of his mother's brother (that is, the daughter of his father-in-law). Only a few societies in the world, such as the Kedang in Indonesia, have a prescriptive system of matrilateral cross-cousin marriage (see Barnes 1974:270). As Needham has defined it in a number of articles, the definitive feature of a matrilateral prescriptive system is a mode of articulation that characterizes the classification as a whole (see Needham 1973). The entire system is designed to make mother's brother's daughter the prescribed wife. The Pakao system, however, has several nonprescriptive equations, such as MBS=FZS and MBD=FZD. These equations are both denoted by the Mandinka word for "cross-cousin" (*sanao*). One of the ironic reasons that the Pakao system falls short of a prescriptive system is that both cross-cousins and parallel cousins are classified as "brothers" (*baringke*). The terminology can thus create nearly as many mother's brother's daughters as is systematically possible without losing the definitional nature of a category.

In the anthropological literature, many studies of kinship terminologies refer only to radical terms (kinship words which are not combinations of smaller words). This is not possible in the Pakao system because some of the most frequently used words, such as those based on "mother," are compound terms. These combine radical terms with certain suffixes or prefixes. Counting both the radical and the compound, there are thirty-one commonly used kinship terms in Pakao. This entire terminological system can be built of the twelve radical terms, six suffixes, and two prefixes contained in Table 3.

TABLE 3   MANDINKA KINSHIP TERMS

Radical Terms

1.	mumu	FFF
2.	mama	FF
3.	fa	F
4.	ba	M
5.	bink	FZ, HM
6.	bitao	WF, WM, HF, HM
7.	koto	eB, eZ
8.	doko	yB, yZ
9.	sanao	MBS, MBD, FZS, FZD
10.	dingo	S, D, BS, BD, ZS, ZD
11.	kema	H
12.	muso	W

Suffixes			Prefixes		
1.	ke	male	1.	fa	patrilateral
2.	muso	female	2.	ba	matrilateral
3.	keba	elder			
4.	ding	younger			
5.	dingo	the child of			
6.	ringo	opposite			

To study the Pakao kinship terms, we are fortunate to have available thirteen word lists dating from the sixteenth through the twentieth centuries.[3] Six of the twelve modern radical terms were recorded in the seventeenth century list (Anonymous 1845).[4] The current modification system of suffixes and prefixes can be found in the same list, and also in the second oldest list compiled by Moore (1738). These portions of the Pakao system have endured for some three centuries. In contrast with continuity, changes in kinship terms are much more difficult to prove, since one can never be sure that an early traveler recorded all the words in use. Supposing that each of the word lists is complete, two trends are evident in the evolution of a kinship terminology. The first, not inconsistent with the values of Islam, is a proliferation of age and sex distinctions for siblings and then for mother's sister and father's brother. The second is a proliferation of compound terms increasingly reflective of matrilateral cross-cousin marriage. Both of these trends, however, might be due exclusively to the improving linguistic skill of the travelers who successively recorded the terms.

AGE-SETS AND INFORMAL GRADES

Age-sets are a means of organizing groups of people by age. In Pakao, the age-sets serve as the basis of work groups and of a naming system that allows members of the same set to call each other "age-mate." There is also an informal system of age-grades, which for the most part lacks clearly defined grades and transitions between them.

The basic structure of the Pakao age-set system is illustrated by defining individual features. The term *sequence* refers to all the age-sets in one village whose members are of the same sex. Each village has two sequences, one male and the other female. Every age-set thus has within the same village a counterpart age-set whose members are of the opposite sex and of the same age-set level. The term *age-mate* is applied by a Mandinko to members of his (her) age-set, to members of the counterpart of his age-set, and to people about his age from other villages irrespective of the exact level of his own age-set.

"Age-mate" is a strong egalitarian concept. The Mandinka word for "age-mate," *fulao*, is derived from the word for "two" (*fulo*) and bears an etymological resemblance to the word for "twin" (*fulandingo*). "Age-mate" is often used in the place of the appropriate kinship word, in order to avoid the differentiation made by kinship terminology according to sex, relative age, and generation. The age-set recruits members without regard to caste. Two persons may call each other age-mate, while differences in their caste make it impossible for their children to marry.

In theory, each time an age-set is inaugurated, about every five years, all the

---

[3] Anonymous (1600s:1845); Moore (1738); Park (1799); Macbriar (1837); Norris (1841); Koelle (1854); Archer (1904); Hopkinson (1911); Nunn (1934); Hamlyn (1935); Gamble (1949); Rowlands (1959); Ashrif and Sidibe (1965).

[4] *Fa* (father), *ba* (mother), *coto* (brother), *din* (child), *queo* (husband), *moussou* (wife).

ascending age-sets move up one level. Sets that are senior to the speaker's are called "upper"; junior sets are called "lower." An age-set is organized initially among subgroups which recruit children from the same hamlet or two adjacent hamlets. A subgroup is formed when a group of uncircumcised children between the ages of roughly four and nine is summoned to the house of a leader they elect by acclamation. The subgroup is named for its leader, who is always of the same sex and from a senior age-set. In the course of time, the subgroups of an age-set merge under one leader whose name is adopted.

A number of facts about age-set structure can be seen in Tables 4 and 5, containing data on the male and female age-set sequences in Dar Silamé. Chronological ages in the survey were estimated by asking informants to date their birth in relation to locally well-known events whose dates could be established. The tables show that young persons begin meeting as subgroups. Then as young men and women, they meet as single age-sets and finally, sometime around age fifty, they stop meeting as an age-set. The tables show a number of irregularities in the age-set system. These include overlapping ages of individuals in successive sets, age-gaps between successive sets, and differences in age-span between counterpart male and

TABLE 4   THE DAR SILAMÉ AGE-SET SYSTEM:
WOMEN'S SEQUENCE (DECEMBER 1974)

Female set level	Number of original subgroups	Estimated number of original members	Number of current members	Age of youngest living member	Age of oldest living member	Age-sets of original subgroup leaders if living	Current meeting status
1	1	17	16	5	8	7	x
2	3	91	74	3	14	5, 9, 9	x
3	1	23	19	10	19	6	x
4	4	50	31	20	23	10, 7, 9, 7	x
5	3	25	19	25	27	9, 10	x-y
6	3	35	14	24	32	9, 8	y
7	3	40	18	34	44	9, 11	x-y
8	3	23	17	41	45		z
9	3	?	19	46	51	11, 14	y
10	2	35	20	50	55		z
11	2	36	7	54	57		z
12	2	38	8	59	64		z
13	3	29	8	60	63	17	z
14	3	30	14	65	69		z
15	3	20	6	74	75		z
16	2	19	5	75?	77?		z
17	2	30	1	82	same		z
18	?	?	0				z
19	?	?	1	90?	same		z
20	?	?	1	97?	same		z

Abbreviations for "Current meeting status:" x = meets in subgroups under individual leaders; y = meets village-wide under one leader; z = no longer meets as an age-set.

TABLE 5   THE DAR SILAMÉ AGE-SET SYSTEM:
MEN'S SEQUENCE (DECEMBER 1974)

Male set level	Number of original subgroups	Estimated number of original members	Number of current members	Age of youngest living member	Age of oldest living member	Age-sets of original subgroup leaders if living	Current meeting status
1	1	13	13	4	9	2	x
2	3	85	48	10	15	4, 4, 4	x-y
3	3	64	45	12	24	8, 6, 5	x-y
4	3	38	17	21	25	10, 6, 5	y
5	3	49	30	26	29	6, 7, 7	y
6	3	60	21	26	35	10, 8, 8	x-y
7	3	35	12	34	43	9, 8, 10	y
8	3	32	20	41	47	12, 11, 10	y
9	3	35	19	45	53	12, 14	y
10	2	26	12	52	55	14	z
11	3	30	13	54	57	14, 14, 14	z
12	2	35	10	54	60		z
13	1	26	4	60	63		z
14	2	22	13	62	69		z
15	3	?	4	72	75	18	z
16	3	40	5	73	76		z
17	2	28	0				z
18	?	?	1	87	same		z
19	?	?	0				z
20	?	?	0				z

Abbreviations for "Current meeting status:" x = meets in subgroups under individual leaders; y = meets village-wide under one leader; z = no longer meets as an age set.

female sets. One cause of these differences is the shifting of some members from one set joined initially to the immediately junior one. Shifting usually takes place from Level 2 to Level 1. Mandinko allow a mother to bring her young child to an age-set meeting after the set has been inaugurated and before the child's eventual age-mates have formed their own set. Mandinko believe strongly that younger children should be associated with older ones. Some mothers with high infant mortality believe that these associations will be medicinally beneficial to their surviving children. Mandinko refer to these younger, late-joining members of an age-set as "attached children." The set "breaks up" when a junior set is formed from it. This explains why there are four sub-groups in age-set F4 (female sequence, Level 4) and only one subgroup in F3. Another cause of irregularity in the system is that the subgroups within an age-set are not inaugurated at the same time. This can be seen in the case of F1 and M1, where only one subgroup has been inaugurated so far. Further unevenness in the system is caused by the rule that women do not become leaders of an age-set until after they establish residence with their husband. The result is that the leaders of sets in the women's sequence are usually older than the leaders of counterpart men's sets.

Structural considerations aside, what services do the age-sets actually perform? The actively meeting sets in both male and female sequences serve as social clubs. Among the four most junior levels, there are relatively frequent meetings for entertainment, at least once a month. The individual subgroups and age-sets of the men's sequence are also summoned to help out with the farming. A farmer who summons an age-set compensates its members with kola nuts, breakfast, and lunch in his field. Male age-sets tend to be called only for weeding or harvesting, when a farmer and his subhamlet cannot manage by themselves. Active age-sets in the women's sequence play a more instrumental role in rice cultivation. They work every day during the ploughing, weeding, and transplanting phases. The leader of a female subgroup or set rotates her workforce according to need in various fields. In both the men's and women's sequences, there is one leader who has authority over the entire sequence. In Dar Silamé, for example, the chief called on sequence leader Ngangsu Lanjang Samaté to supervise all the male sets during two days of weeding and burning around the village to clear a protective barrier against dry-season brush fires. Mandonko Maria, the leader of the women's

Karantaba: An age-set of women collectively work the soil of a rice field with characteristically long-handled hoes.

sequence in Dar Silamé, had overall authority for age-sets in the ricefields, and was consulted on the bearing and raising of children.

There is also an informal age-grade system, more appropriately thought of as a system of status categories. Among men and women, the most obvious of these categories are "uncircumcised," "circumcised," and "elder." The circumcision ritual marks the transition between the first two categories. There are no stated rules linking membership in a particular age-set with eligibility for circumcision. In age-sets M2 and F2 there were both circumcised and uncircumcised boys and girls; members of the most junior sets were all uncircumcised. After circumcision, there were no more transitions involving the ritual movement of whole groups of people into new statuses. The category "circumcised" (*kintao*) includes everyone through elder who has been through the ceremony, and it also means guardian, those youths and maidens who supervise the uncircumcised during the circumcision ritual. After circumcision, only one more status, "elder," serves as the basis for a group. Among men, the status refers to the elders who sit together at mosque and at ritual meetings, and who are summoned by the chief to hear disputes. There is no formal transition marking entry into this elders council. Individuals, rather than groups, join simply by being asked by a member to sit with the collected membership during a meeting. There is no rule linking a precise level of age-set with membership. The council includes only some men from M11, as well as all the men from M12 and more senior sets. Similarly, women join their elders group one at a time and at the invitation of members. The women's group meets for prayers outside the mosque fence; during circumcision and other rituals they tend to mingle with younger women.

The Pakao age statuses do not work together as a coherent system of defined age-grades, and they do not work in conjunction with the age-set system in any articulated way. The Pakao example seems to contradict the theoretical observation by Stewart that where age-sets are found to be a prominent feature of social organization, "they operate in conjunction with an age-grade system" (1972:126). There is evidence suggesting that the mixture of age-sets and ill-defined grades in Pakao may have evolved from a well-organized age-grade system. Charest describes an age-grade system among a non-Muslim Mandinka group near Kédougou in eastern Senegal (1971:131–156). There are eight grades for men and seven for women. Significantly, the uncircumcised and elder's categories in both the Pakao and Kédougou systems are known by virtually the same words.[5] We also know that the two groups originated from the same ethnic stock and have several of the same clan names. Charest observes two trends that suggest the origin of the Pakao system. First, the Islamization of a few non-Muslim Kédougou villages is bringing about the collapse of the age-grade system (1971:134, 140). Secondly, a system is beginning to emerge in which groups of young men sell their services to work on various projects (Charest 1971:155). These relatively individualistic work groups are replacing the collective agricultural system, and they bear a resemblance to the work-oriented age-sets in Pakao.

---

[5] In Pakao, "uncircumcised" is *solima;* in Kédougou it is *soliman-lu.* In Pakao, "elder" is *keba;* in Kédougou it is *sukeba.*

CIRCUMCISION

The Mandinko circumcise both girls and boys. The circumcision for either sex is most commonly referred to by the same Mandinka word, *kwiyung*. For this reason, I call the ceremony by the nearest English equivalent, *circumcision*. The operation, of course, varies. For boys, the foreskin is removed from the penis. For girls, the entire clitoris is removed.

The ritual of circumcision is a focal point in the lives of Mandinka children. From an early age, they look forward to the secretive ritual with fear and curiosity. Surreptitiously, they try to find out what the ritual will be like, and they are teased about their status as uncircumcised. The oldest uncircumcised boy and girl in a village are singled out for the brunt of the teasing. Among the Mandinko, the youngest boys in one circumcised group might be older than boys held back by their parents until the next circumcision. A circumcision song captures the awkwardness of this situation: "There were two children. The younger was circumcised first. The elder was circumcised later. The younger will always be the guardian of his 'older brother'."

Circumcision is important to the Mandinko in very basic ways. The experience is a prerequisite for attaining adult status and is necessary in order to marry. In the society of today, a woman waits from three to five years after circumcision before marrying, and a man will wait ten years or more. Mandinko say that in the past a girl married right after circumcision. Mungo Park observed this in the late eighteenth century (1969:203, 204). He also noted a belief among non-Muslim Mandinko that circumcision improved fertility. I asked Queen Koto Fadera why the Mandinko circumcise, and she replied, "This is what has always been done, ever since the Mandinko came from Manding."

I shall begin with an account of male circumcision and then proceed to the female ritual. A boys' circumcision is held roughly every five years. Mandinka novices range from about age six to thirteen. Two ceremonies in early 1975 involved average-sized groups of thirty and forty-six boys. The timing of a circumcision ritual is important to the symbolism of fertility and of the passage into adulthood. The ceremony takes place in late December or early January after the harvest has been completed. This facilitates the construction of the lodge, which is built of millet stalks. Millet, a men's crop, certainly predates the peanuts introduced in the mid-nineteenth century and is said by Mandinka elders to be primordial. Other advantages to the timing of circumcision were suggested. Since the ritual is held after the harvest, the boys' absence from the fields is not missed. The rice harvest is also finished, and women no longer spend much time away from the village. This means that the male novices, living in and around the lodge, have fewer opportunities to see a woman during seclusion. If they do, they are beaten.

A boys' circumcision is convened by the village chief, a circumcisor living in the village or some other prominent elder. The day of circumcision begins at dawn for the novice. He is carried to the place of circumcision on the shoulders of a guardian, an "older brother" who went through a previous ceremony. Just prior to circumcision, the village men file out by hamlet to the spot. After some reflective waiting, each boy is circumcised while sitting at the edge of a hole with

Soumboundou: Moments after the novices have been circumcised in a nearby field, their guardians race back to the village and, kicking up a cloud of dust, joyously perform the leaf dance.

his legs spread around it. As explained by Ibrahima Danfa, a circumcisor of Soumboundou, the foreskin must be buried "to prevent cannibal-witches from finding it." He added that the foreskin "is a part of the body and hence ought to be buried." In some villages, for example Karantaba, Mankono, and Soumboundou, the novice is circumcised with his father standing on his right and his mother's brother on his left. In Dar Silamé, each novice is circumcised while he leans against a small tree called his mother's brother. The guardian helps to clot the blood with the outside covering of a millet stalk. Later, the novice uses one of several remedies to heal the wound. He attaches a leaf of *pelinkumfo* or the bark of the *batio* around his penis.[6] A Western ointment might also be used. After circumcision, a few guardians remain with the novices, and the others race joyously back to the village waving branches. This is the "leaf dance." Singing songs and dancing, the young people circle the village, passing through all the hamlets and subhamlets. The celebration of unity is reflected in the words of a leaf dance song: "The *fara* tree and the *jambakatao*; all for one and one for all."[7]

---

[6] *Pelinkumfo (Aframomum sceptrum); batio (Nauclea latifolia).*

[7] *Fara (Piliostigma thongii); jambakatao (Combretum glutinosum).* Keba Dramé explained that these two plants symbolize a unity of man and nature because both are relied on by people. The *fara* tree is continually stripped of bark to make the *kangkurao*. The *jambakatao*, literally "bitter leaf," is one of the most popular purgative medicines.

Around midday, the guardians and older men begin constructing the lodge under a large, sacred tree. In Soumboundou the lodge is traditionally built under a great *tabo*.[8] In Mankono and Karantaba the novices are circumcised around massive old *tabo* trees. The *tabo* is easily the most sacred of all trees in Pakao. The demon-spirits sheltered in its branches protect the novice by killing off or driving away evil cannibal-witches.

A *kangkurao* mask is brought out to the site where the lodge is being constructed, to compel the workers to finish the task by nightfall. The novices enter the lodge in the evening and begin a period of seclusion and recuperation that lasts from one and a half to two months. The novices are dressed in white costumes with hoods to shield their foreheads, since they are considered vulnerable to cannibal-witches. They all carry large square charms especially designed by *marabouts* to ward off evil spirits. From the beginning of seclusion, there is a somewhat fearful atmosphere in the lodge, fostered by occasional beatings. The novices subserviently follow the instructions of the lodge chief and their guardians, who live in the lodge with them. They are taught to act as a cohesive group, and they do virtually everything in the lodge collectively. The novices take all their meals together, beginning and ending on the signal of the lodge chief. Each morning they go together in single file to the secret place of plant healing. Each

[8] *Tabo (Cola cordifolia).*

Missera: Singing circumcision songs in the lodge, the novices keep time by tapping the railing in the central corridor.

afternoon they gather firewood that is sent back to the cooking fires of their mothers. In the evenings they spend hours singing call-and-response songs with their guardians. Often in amusing and symbolic fashion, the circumcision songs illustrate values of the society, such as respect for elders and a sexual tension between men and women. One song likens a girl to a rabbit. "There is a rabbit at at the edge of the village. Soro greets her and complains that she doesn't budge. Others criticize her for moving too fast."

Circumcision points the novice toward adulthood and marriage, and initiates a transition in the nature of kinship relations. Prior to the ritual, boys are sternly disciplined by their fathers, and there is little cohesiveness among brothers. Many boys will not have developed any systematic contact with their mother's brother. The circumcision and seclusion signal the beginning of a reciprocal and sometimes affectionate respect for the elder brother, the father, and the mother's brother.

Mandinko state that the socializing force in the lodge is fear. Nambaly Sagnan, a lodge chief in Dar Silamé, said that when a novice will not stop crying, he calls in a *kangkurao*. The *kangkurao* enters the lodge and sometimes beats the novice with the flat edge of his machete. At night, Mandinka lodge chiefs use two additional demon-spirits to discipline the novices, the *ngarankulo* and the *jalikono*.

Missera: The novices plunge into the upper Soungrougrou River for "River-wash." They ritually wash themselves for the first time in the two weeks since their circumcision.

To make the *ngarankulo*, a guardian stands outside the lodge and whirls a bull-roarer. The *jalikono* is portrayed by a guardian who stands in a tree and burns palm fronds, causing a spectacular shower of sparks. Near the end of seclusion the novices are taught how to fabricate these demon-spirits.

There are four principal stages marking the period of seclusion. About two weeks after circumcision, the novices go to an event called "river-washing," either at a river or a water hole in the forest. The novices wash themselves and their clothes for the first time since circumcision. This is a form of ritual purification and practical cleanliness, demonstrating that the novices are well enough to undertake the difficulties of a footrace that afternoon. The footrace, called *samaso* ("snatch the hat"), is run in two heats and is about 100 yards long. A third stage occurs near the end of seclusion and is marked by a feast for the novices prepared by their mothers. The novices line up and the mothers, bringing out the food, see them for the first time since circumcision. The display suggests the polite distance that will characterize the future relation between mother and son. The final stage of seclusion is the burning down of the lodge at night by the guardians, at which time the novices return home.

Taking place after the rice harvest, the timing of the girls' circumcision parallels that of boys and evokes similar images of maturation. The girls are carried to circumcision on the backs of "older sisters," the guardians. This means of transportation is said to mimic a mother carrying her baby, and symbolizes the close relation that will exist between younger and elder sister, and between novice and guardian during seclusion. The novice wears a dark blue skirt and smock. She is blindfolded with a scarf draped over her head. The place of circumcision is marked by a large tree. In Dar Silamé circumcision takes place under a *tabo* tree. In Soumboundou, Karantaba, and other villages, the *jungo* and the *jalo*[9] mark the site. These are considered women's trees. *Jungo* is used to make the handle of a woman's rice hoe. *Jalo* is used in making a mortar, the pestle, and the stool used by women in the cook-house.

The clitoridectomy is performed by an elder woman, either a specialist in circumcision or the circumcision queen herself (who also convenes the ceremony and supervises the seclusion). One by one, the novices sit at the edge of the same hole, with their legs spread around it. The novice faces the circumcisor as the operation is performed. Each novice is held by a reassuring elder woman (of no particular kinship) seated behind her. The guardians and elder women help the novices apply boiled bandages and inexpensive Western ointments. The girls are then secluded in the queen's house for ten to fifteen days. Koto Fadera said that for a large group of novices she had constructed a girls' lodge of palm fronds, located in the garden near her house.

As in the male seclusion, the girls live with their guardians and are taught to work together as a group. They similarly learn the values of the society by singing call-and-response songs with the guardians. A typical song emphasizes the virtue of hard work: "Get your work clothes; let's go to the rice fields." The first two stages of girls' seclusion are the same as those in the boys' ritual. Riverwashing

---

[9] *Jungo (Mitragyna inermis); jalo (Khaya senegalensis).*

Soumboundou: Howa is carried by her older sister. Like many African peoples, the Mandinko carry babies and young children on their backs. This enables the mothers to carry their children while performing household chores or even culti- vating rice. Informants say that the only disadvantage to the system is that children frequently do not learn to walk until they are at least two or three years old.

and the novice's footrace are held for the same reasons. To mark a third phase of seclusion, the girl novices are given a feast and are permitted to ask for any food they want. There is no display of the girls to their fathers. The seclusion ends with dancing. The girls' lodge is, of course, not burned. This structure is the queen's house, and burning it would endanger the village.

Structural similarities between the male and female rituals, concerning purpose, phases, and timing, suggest a conceptual equivalence of the sexes. There are nevertheless important qualitative differences. Girls are circumcised in smaller groups than boys, ranging from one to fifteen or twenty. Girls' circumcisions are held more frequently than boys', perhaps every two or three years. The period of seclusion is shorter. Girls say that not much hazing takes place during their seclusion, and there are no fabricated demon-spirits. The girls' seclusion is a less violent experience and is probably less fearful. The queen plays a relatively more dominant role. Since she has no demon-spirits to command, she has to rely more on her own prowess to protect the girls from cannibal-witches. As a result, the bond between the girl novice and the queen is comparatively strong. There is also an important relationship between the girl novices and the elder women assisting the queen. No parallel relation exists in the male lodge. The girls' circumcision ritual establishes a source of power for the queen, validating her leadership and on-going authority over the village women. In contrast, the male lodge chief has no authority outside of the ritual context.

The Mandinka circumcision ritual is not free of the pressures of modernization. In a few villages near Sédhiou and in Sédhiou itself, boys are sent to the local clinic to be circumcised. *Kangkurao* are still summoned, however, and other parts of the ritual such as the leaf dance are performed, in the streets if necessary. In Mankono Ba, one group of boys was circumcised in the summer so that their seclusion would not interfere with school. The novices were secluded in the village. This altered approach to circumcision angered some of the men, who argued that subsequent rituals would be carried out according to tradition.

THE *KANGKURAO*

The cult of the *kangkurao* is a baffling institution, considering the devotion of Pakao Muslims to Islam. The mask contradicts the values of orthodox Islam in several ways. It is a graven image. Its violence has nothing to do with the militant advance of Islam. In most cases the mask is brought out by the young men of a village, temporarily taking away the authority of the all-powerful elders of the mosque. Finally, the *kangkurao* is fanatically believed to be omnipotent by a people who insist that Allah is their "one and only king."

Surely such contradictions are sufficient to put an end to this masked cult. Trimingham concludes that this trend has been generally true in West Africa. He writes that in cases where masks continue to operate in Islamized societies, they no longer have socioreligious significance, they may degenerate into a form of clowning, and their material symbols are neglected (1959:38). To the contrary, the Pakao *kangkurao* is flourishing and is deadly serious business. The institution has also spread to adjacent ethnic groups such as the Balant and the Jola. In Pakao, Islam should have had ample time since the 1840s to bring about the demystification of the mask. Why has this not happened?

A functional explanation for the persistence of the *kangkurao* is its importance to contemporary social organization. It is no exaggeration to say that the *kangkurao* plays a major role in social control. To this end, I observed it performing a variety of functions. *Kangkurao* were used to enforce the digging of wells. In Mankono Ba, one was even used to conscript and to supervise a workforce during the construction of a cement wall around the mosque. *Kangkurao* routinely placed prohibitions against eating mangoes and oranges until the fruit matured. In Soumboundou, the *kangkurao* exacted a heavy fine from the chief and the *imam* after their sons broke the prohibition. A *kangkurao* was brought out to enforce mass participation in the fire prevention weeding around Dar Silamé. *Kangkurao* were also used during circumcision and seclusion and to discipline the novices, to supervise construction of the lodge, and to drive away spectators from other villages.

A more intellectual reason for the *kangkurao's* persistence is its place in Mandinka thought. The *kangkurao* sets up some of the basic oppositions in the Pakao society and helps to maintain borders between them. It has a special antipathy towards women and uncircumcised children. After one of its masquerades through Dar Silamé, the bark coat of the *kangkurao* was hung in a tree not far from the village. It was placed there as a warning to women and children that the wishes of the escorting group must be followed out, or else the *kangkurao* would be

Mankono Ba: Youths of the escorting group, some of them terrified, kneel to receive a beating from the bark-clad kangkurao.

brought to life again. One youth threatened emotionally that "if uncircumcised girls see the bark, or if women investigate it, the *kangkurao* will reappear and put them to death."

To Mandinko, social control can also occur at a magical level. A demon-spirit is one of the major forces capable of killing a cannibal-witch, and the *kangkurao* is the most lethal of these spirits. *Kangkurao* are frequently used for this purpose during circumcision and seclusion. The *kangkurao* system thus proves the ability of human beings to exert a final control over demon-spirits and other forces of the unknown. A *kangkurao* cannot appear on its own. It has to be summoned by a principal of the village, usually a chief, an *imam*, or a lodge chief. The elder must assign it a mission to carry out. This is a civilizing act towards a dangerous and volatile force capable of bringing death and destruction to humans. Endowed with a purpose, the *kangkurao* as demon-spirit can be a beneficial force, and the youth who escort it will not misuse their power in destructive fashion.

There is probably something of a historical inertia behind the durability of the *kangkurao*. During four centuries travelers to the Senegambia have recorded masked figures in detail, and the principles of social order they embody are quite similar to those of the modern *kangkurao*. Over a long period of time these principles have acquired a weight and motion of their own, so that a *kangkurao* is entwined with the very definition of the society. In the early seventeenth century, Jobson reported a figure known as *Ho-re*. This spirit made a terrifying noise, like all modern demon-spirits, but had no costume or other physical presence. Paralleling the *kangkurao*, it was an agent of violence and social control, prone to vent its wrath against uncircumcised boys (1968:147–151). In the early 1700s, Francis Moore described a mask called the *mumbo jumbo* (1738:40, 116, 117, 133). The name of this mask has passed into English and of course now refers to black magic, hocus-pocus, or any complicated language that obscures and confuses.[10] The *mumbo jumbo* resembled a *kangkurao* in several ways. It wore a bark coat and was designed to mystify women, resolving all disputes with them in favor of men. The mask wearer was attended by a group of males who carried out its wishes violently. Those who gained knowledge of the mask were sworn never to tell women or boys under the age of 15. The *mumbo jumbo* described by Mungo Park in the late eighteenth century is also similar to the *kangkurao* (1969:29, 30). Its bark costume was hung in the bough of a tree. The mask was used mainly by non-Muslims to discipline women and, on one occasion witnessed by Park, did so with a violent beating. Today, such corporeal punishment by a *kangkurao* is more of an implied threat to women and is, in effect, no longer meted out. In the early 1800s, Dochard and Gray reported two masks, a *mumbo jumbo* and a *kong-corong* (1825:55, 82). The latter apparently bears the name of the modern *kang-kurao*, although it was made of tree leaves rather than bark. Both masks were

---

[10] *Mumbo jumbo* may have come into English via the slave trade or through its appearance in popular eighteenth-century explorers' accounts by Francis Moore (1738) and Mungo Park (1969). The adoption of African words into English is a fascinating topic and has caused some interesting debate. For example, the linguist David Dalby argues that the origin of the familiar *O.K.* might be traced to similar Mandinka or Wolof terms passed on through the slave trade (1970:23). During my fieldwork, the Mandinko used *okay, okae, okay kuta*, and *okay kuta baki* to indicate agreement in the same way that *O.K.* is used in English.

instruments of social control against women. The appearance of either mask was also an occasion for singing and dancing.

In historical context, the *kangkurao* is more than an agent of social control over both the physical and the magical world. It represents a structural system enduring over time. Despite outward fluctuations and adaptations, its basic principles have a proven longevity and are a force of cultural continuity. The institution of the *kangkurao* tends to defend the status quo, and in recent times at least, has taken on an element of resistance. Nambaly Sagnan of Dar Silamé once told me that if whites ever tried to interfere with a circumcision, he would call in *kangkurao* to kill them. In Karantaba, the chief's son told of an incident involving a particularly dangerous sort of *kangkurao* called a *fangbondi* (meaning "it brings itself out"). As suggested literally by its name, this mask has no escorting group. It physically resembles a *kangkurao* but has the added capability of flight. Swearing that his account was true, the chief's son said that a district administrator visited Karantaba in the 1960s to investigate a complaint by a woman that she had been beaten by a *fangbondi*. The beating caused her to have a miscarriage. The chief was detained but was either unwilling or unable to give out a mask-wearer's name. A search party from Karantaba was sent to find the bark costume in the forest. They returned and threw it on the ground in front of the administrator. The *fangbondi* suddenly sprang to life and severely beat the administrator. It even prevented him from escaping in his car. The administrator allegedly sent word to Pakao chiefs that if a *fangbondi* ever killed anyone, he did not want to know about it.

Epilogue: Mandinka democracy

The reader may have gathered the impression that Mandinka society still tends to institutionalize inequality with its caste system and dominant religious elders. This epilogue provides an opportunity to reflect broadly on the Mandinka political system and to argue that it is more democratic than it seems.

When President Nixon resigned because of Watergate, I was in the village of Soumboundou and heard the news on a Voice of America broadcast. This was news that had to be shared. I found my host, Chief Jeta Camera, sitting on his bamboo platform and, under sparkling evening stars, proceeded to explain the recent events to him. To do so, I had to explain something of American politics, and in translation my list of presidents sounded more like a genealogy of leader-heroes. The chief was delighted that a man so powerful could fall from power, for Nixon's reputation seemed to him very much like Mandinka kingship (*mansaya*). The chief concluded that "Nixon was like a king (*mansa*) and he fell from power because of evil deeds." The Mandinka appreciation of this situation is not difficult to understand. To the devout Muslims of Pakao, kings are infidels. Kingship implies a dangerous excess of power and much more. It lacks the proper spirituality and is unaccountable, repressive, and intolerant. In turn, Mandinka political virtues are piety, generosity, responsiveness, and truthfulness. As related previously, the Mandinko themselves often define their political system negatively as one of nonkingship. The *jihad* leader Syllaba "was not a king." In myths, both Syllaba and his son Fodali Sylla renounce the kingship that may have been within their grasp. The anathema of kingship among Mandinko is an egalitarian concept, and it helps to raise a fundamental question

Is Mandinka society democratic in the sense of favoring social equality, disallowing social exclusiveness, and giving power to the common man? Certainly there are both autocratic and undemocratic structures in the society. Only elders can hold positions of authority. There are slaves, and they are considered of low status. The caste system does not allow marriage between castes. There are exclusive divisions of social organization between men and women, who indeed have separate age-sets and circumcision rituals; the women have their *dembajasa* society, and the men have the cult of the *kangkurao*. The chief has final and independent authority in decision making that relates to the physical welfare of the village, and the same is true of the *imam* with respect to the village's spiritual well-being. Among women, the queen can be even more autocratic. She is, after all, called a

105

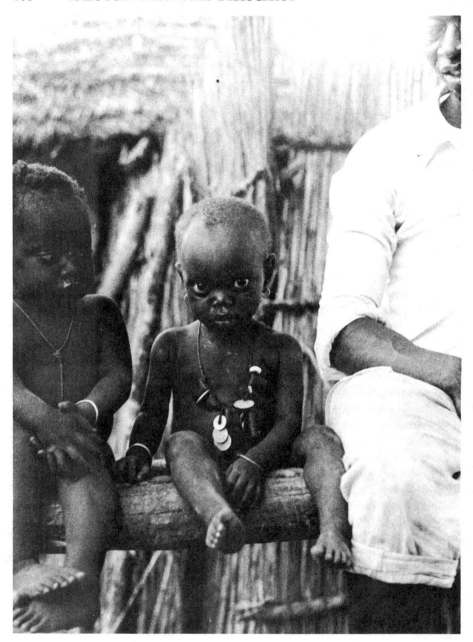

Mankono Ba: An infant girl with a necklace of protective charms.

"queen," and her counterpart among men is despised in theory and no longer exists in practice.

Despite the exclusive groupings among the Mandinko and the potential for autocratic leadership, I would say that the society is strongly democratic in the sense of providing for social equality. In effect, the Mandinko have a system of minimal government. Chiefs do not govern but are available to make decisions in case they are needed. The villages of Pakao consider themselves a polity but have no jurisdiction of leadership greater than the level of a village The minimal system allows groups of people to have greater influence. The council of the elders meets frequently, and the chief never makes an important decision without convening it. The only criterion for membership in the council is the subjective concept "elder"; caste makes no difference. Age-sets enhance the influence of younger groups of people. The *kangkurao* gives the young men a real power in the society. The Mandinko have a great love of argument and whenever there are meetings of the elders' council, age-sets, or the *kangkurao* group, the relevant issues are vigorously debated.

In general, strong leadership has been most notable when the society apparently needed it—during the upheaval of the *jihad* and the later confrontations with the colonial government. The age requirement for chief is applied simply, so that any noble male of the founding hamlet can become chief if he lives long enough, regardless of wealth or some other criterion. The *imam* is not only an elected official; his authority can be a balance to that of the chief. It is true that the society provides no parallel and countervailing authority in relation to the queen. However, her position can be filled by a woman of low status (for example, a slave), and her unique power helps to guarantee women's freedom from domination by men. The exclusive divisions in the ritual and social organizations of men and women further strengthen the independence of women. These equalizing mechanisms are especially useful in the religious context. While Islam serves as a powerful democratizing force among men by diminishing caste differences, it is also perhaps the most significant force available to men to facilitate their control over women. Only men can become *marabouts*, controlling both the mosque and the dispensing of Islamic charms which women purchase in profusion.

Within the more formal Mandinka social organization, there is also room for the independence and initiative of the *kanda* and the entrepreneur. The Mandinko admire their aggressiveness but nevertheless consider it a virtue only when blended with temperence and reason. The latter are qualities that usually win out in the many debates, and a person who has them can be rewarded with a great compliment. It is said, according to a Mandinka idiom, that "he has a good liver." In the final analysis, the mixture of Mandinka personality, social philosophy, and religion makes it possible for the undemocratic mechanisms in the society to operate in a larger democratic context.

Glossary of Mandinka terms

alimamo: imam

alkalo: chief

arajena: heaven

asan: to sell; also, to buy

Bainuk: pejorative for non-Muslim; also, an ethnic group

Bakao bada bada: Pakao forever and ever

balafong: a wooden xylophone with wooden resonators

baring: mother's brother; also, wife's father

bwa: the cannibal-witch, a person who takes on an animal shape to harm others; also, owl

dembajasa: a woman who changes her name and dances occasionally as a transvestite, so that her offspring will be spared by evil spirits; literally "clowning mother"

dua: a powerful prayer of intercession; also, a curse

dumasu: lower village

fa: to kill; also, to die

fangbondi: a particularly dangerous type of *kangkurao* that can fly and that is never escorted by a group of youths; literally, "brings itself out"

faroto: rice fields

fino: a type of praise-singer who chants his praise, calling out honorific names and reciting lists of characters from the Koran

fulandingo: twin

fulao: age-mate

fulo: two

gino: demon-spirits, which can kill or harm people and also destroy the evil cannibal-witch

hadiso: the type of praise chanted by the *fino*

jahanama: hell

jalikono: a type of demon-spirit portrayed by a man who stands in a tree at night and burns palm fronds, showering sparks to the ground

jalo: all types of praise-singer

jamingo:. mosque

jatti: host

joka: a type of praise-singer who invents rhymed phrases and sings them, often accompanied by a drummer

jubero: oracle; also, seeing

julo: trader, merchant

jungo: slave caste

kabilo: hamlet within a village (major lineage)

kaburo: grave, cemetery

kafotonyoma: friend, member of the same group

kanda: a particularly wealthy and influential man

kangkurao: a demon-spirit in which a mask-wearer covers his entire body with blood-red bark

karanke: leatherworker

keba: elder

kintao: circumcision guardian; also, everyone who has been circumcised

konton: clan name; also, to greet

kora: a stringed instrument with a large resonator made from a skin stretched over a gourd

korda: subhamlet (minor lineage)

kulio: infant's naming ceremony, literally "head shaving"

kumfanute: wizard, literally "wide head," a person who can foretell the future, perceive evil cannibal-witches, and if necessary, change into an animal form to accomplish a mission

kungkoto: peanut and millet fields

kuro: age-set (Pakao Mandinko)

kwiyungo (kwiyung):   circumcision ceremony

luntao: guest, stranger, outsider, foreigner (in effect, everyone not descended from the founding, chiefly lineage of a village)

mansa: king

mansaya: kingship

manyo: bride during the seclusion period when she is ritually transferred from her father's to her husband's people

marabout (French):   local Islamic cleric who combines magical and religious functions (*moro* in Mandinko)

misero: prayer house

mumbo jumbo: a type of masked figure (described during the eighteenth and nineteenth centuries) resembling a *kangkurao* and used to control women and children

munko: ceremonial white rice dough; also, funeral

muso mansa: queen or circumcision queen

ngansungo: the novice during circumcision and seclusion

ngarankulo: a type of demon-spirit portrayed with a bull-roarer at night

nio: soul

numo: smith

nyamalo: artisan—praise-singer caste

okay, okae, okay kuta, and *okay kuta baki:*   o.k.

safo: charm, written charm

salo: prayer (said five times daily)

samaso: the footrace of circumcision novices

sanao: cross-cousin; also, hamlet ally; also, clan with whom one has joking relations

sano: gold

santosu: upper village

singa: purgatory, between heaven and hell

solima: the uncircumcised

soninke: non-Muslim (pejorative)

sula: noble caste

sungo: fasting

suokono: household; also, the village, as distinguished from the fields

tabala: summoning drum emblematic of chiefly authority

tubabo: white man

ulokono: forest; also, forest and peanut/millet fields, as distinguished from the village

Glossary of technical terms

Affinal: refers to kinship that results from marriage (that is, relatives by marriage).
Age-grades: consecutive levels or status through which whole groups of people pass successively.
Age-mate: a fellow member of one's age-set.
Age-set: ideally, a closed group of people of roughly the same age who remain together as a group throughout life.
Bifurcation: division of a whole unit of society into two parts (for example, the division of a village into "upper" and "lower" parts).
Bride Gift: payment made by a husband to his wife as part of the confirmation of the marriage.
Bride Price: payment made by a man to his wife's people as part of marriage negotiations.
Caste: in Pakao, a group of people formerly of a certain station in life and associated with certain professions (for instance, slaves, artisan–praise-singers). Today caste is relevant mainly as an endogamous group: intermarriage is not permitted between castes and is allowed only within the caste.
Clan: people of the same family name wherever they are found.
Classificatory: refers to kinsmen related by category of kinship term. For example, all the men of one's hamlet and of the same generation are one's "brothers."
Cross-cousin: cousins whose related parents are of the opposite sex (someone's father's sister's child, someone's mother's brother's child).
Endogamous: forbidding marriage outside a defined group. See *caste*.
Exchange: in a marriage context, the tendency of the women of one hamlet to be married to the men of another hamlet and vice versa.
Exogamous: forbidding marriage within a defined group. See *hamlet*.
Fallow: to leave a field in a wild, uncultivated state for a period of time, in order to permit the soil to be replenished naturally by the build-up of organic matter.
Genealogical (as distinguished from classificatory):   refers to kinsmen related by blood and belonging to the same immediate (or nuclear) family.
Genealogy: a list of direct descendants. More generally, a list or diagram of people showing the kinship among them.
Hamlet: in Pakao, ideally a specific area of houses within a village, containing men of the same clan name and their families. The hamlet acts as an exogamous group and can be equated with a "major lineage." See *lineage*.
Joking Relations: a formal system of friendship between two clans, that permits familiar behavior such as joking and is sometimes encouraging to marriage.
Lineage: a descent group or a group of people descended from a common ancestor. A "major lineage" is those men (and their families) in a village with the same family name and who are an exogamous group. See *hamlet*. A "minor lineage" is genealogical brothers and their families. See *subhamlet*.

111

Matrilateral: kinship determined through the mother and her brothers or sisters.

Matrilateral Cross-cousin: someone's mother's brother's child.

Matrilateral Cross-cousin Marriage: a system of marriage in which a man marries his mother's brother's daughter (his matrilateral cross-cousin).

Patrilateral: kinship determined through the father and his brothers or sisters.

Patrilateral Cross-cousin: someone's father's sister's child.

Patrilineal: descent determined through the male line.

Parallel Cousin: cousins whose related parents are of the same sex (someone's father's brother's child, someone's mother's sister's child).

Polygamy: a system that permits a man to be married to more than one wife at a time.

Preferential: in the context of a marriage system, this refers to the stated preference for a certain relative as a wife (such as the matrilateral cross-cousin). In the case of Pakao, numerical evidence reveals that the matrilateral cross-cousin was in fact married more often than other categories of relatives.

Prescriptive: refers to a marriage system in which rules prescribe that a certain category of relative, such as the matrilateral cross-cousin, must always be selected as a wife. Rules also prescribe that certain relatives must not be married. The nature of the kinship terminology and, indeed, a whole system of symbolic values support the concept of a prescription.

Sedentary: refers to a people or society remaining in one place for a long time, as opposed to wandering.

Siblings: someone's brothers and sisters.

Subhamlet: in Pakao, ideally a specific area of houses within a hamlet containing genealogical brothers and their families. A subhamlet can be equated with a "minor lineage." See *lineage*.

Totemism: the practice of associating a clan of people with an animal or some natural or manmade object. The totem is "respected" by the clan and is thus not harmed or touched.

Bibliography

Alvares d'Almada, André. 1946. *Tratado breve dos rios de Guiné*. Lisbon: Silveira.

Anonymous (d'Avezac?). 1845. Notice sur le pays et le peuple des Yébous en Afrique. *Mémoires de la Société Ethnologique* 2: 1–267.

Anonymous (Mrs. Hannah Kilham?). 1828. *Specimens of African Languages Spoken in the Colony of Sierra Leone*. London: White.

Archer, Francis Risset. 1904. *The Gambia Colony and Protectorate: An Official Handbook*. London: St. Bride's Press.

Ashrif, M. I., and Sidibe, B. 1965. *English–Mandinka Dictionary*. Yundum. (Volume consulted in The School of Oriental and African Studies, London.)

Barnes, R. H. 1974. *Kédang: A Study of the Collective Thought of an Eastern Indonesian People*. Oxford: Clarendon.

De Barros, Joam. 1932. *Asia de Joam de Barros*. (Edited by Antonio Baião.) Coimbra.

Bertrand-Bocandé, M. 1849. Notes sur la Guinée portugaise ou Sénégambie mériodionale. *Bulletin de la Société de Géographie* 12 (65–66, 67–68): 265–350, 57–93.

Bonnel de Mézières, M. A. 1949. Les Diakhanké de Banisiraila et du Boundou méridional (Sénégal). *Bulletin de l'Information et de Correspondance de l'IFAN* 41: 20–24.

Boulègue, J. 1968. La Sénégambie du milieu du XVe siècle au début du XVIIe siècle. Unpublished Ph.D. thesis, Université de Paris, Faculté des Lettres et Sciences Humaines.

Caillé, R. 1830. *Journal d'un voyage à Temboctou et à Jenné*. Paris: l'Imprimerie Royale.

Cissoko, S-K., and Sambou, K. 1969. Recueil des traditions orales des Mandingues de Gambie et de Casamance. Dakar: Typescript volume in the IFAN library.

Charest, Paul. 1969. Relations inter-ethniques et développement dans l'agglomération de Nyemeneki–Segueko–Touba Diakha. *Bulletins et Mémoires de la Société d'Anthropologie de Paris* 5: 101–229.

———. 1971. Les échelons d'age chez les Malinké de Kédougou (Sénégal oriental). In Denise Paulme (ed.), *Classes et Associations d'Âge en Afrique de l'Ouest*. Paris: Plon, pp. 131–156.

Clarke, J. 1972. *Specimens of Dialects*. (Edited by Edwin Ardener; first published, 1848.) Gregg International.

Curtin, Philip D. 1969. *The Atlantic Slave Trade: A Census*. Madison: University of Wisconsin.

———. 1975. *Economic Change in Precolonial Africa*. Madison: University of Wisconsin.

Cust, Robert Needham. 1883. *A Sketch of the Modern Languages of Africa*. London: Trubner.

Dalby, David. 1970. *Black through White: Patterns of Communication,* Hans Wolff Memorial Lecture. Bloomington, Ind.: Indiana University.

―――. 1971. Distribution and nomenclature of the Manding people and their language. In Carleton T. Hodge (ed.), *Papers on the Manding.* The Hague, The Netherlands: Mouton, pp. 1–13.

Dawood, N. J. (trans.). 1974. *The Koran.* Penguin Books.

Delafosse, Maurice. 1913. Mots Sudanais du moyen âge. *Mémoires de la Société de Linguistique de Paris* 18: 281–288.

―――. 1929. *La Langue Mandingue et ses Dialectes (Malinké, Bambara, Dioula),* Vol. 1. Paris: Geuthner.

―――. 1955. *La Langue Mandingue et ses Dialectes (Malinké, Bambara, Dioula),* Vol. 2. Paris Geuthner.

Dochard, and Gray, William. 1825. *Travels in Western Africa.* London: Murray.

Douglas, Mary. 1970. *Natural Symbols.* London: Cresset.

Evans-Pritchard, E. E. 1940. *The Nuer.* Oxford: Clarendon Press.

Fernandes, Valemtim. 1951. *Description de la Côte Occidentale d'Afrique (Sénégal au Cap de Monte Archipels).* Edited by T. Monod, A. Texeira da Mota, and R. Mauny). Bissau: Centro de Estudos da Guiné Portuguesa.

Gamble, D. P. 1949. *Mandinka–English Dictionary.* London: Research Department, Colonial Office.

―――. 1955. *Economic Conditions in Two Mandinka Villages—Kerewan and Keneba.* London: Research Department, Colonial Office.

―――. 1956. *Mandinka Reading Book.* Bathurst: Government Printer.

Girard, J. 1965. Diffusion en milieu Diola de l'association du *koumpo* Bainouk. *Bulletin de l'IFAN* 27: 42–98.

Glass, D. V. (ed.). 1971. *Social Mobility in Britain.* (First published, 1954.) London: Routledge & Kegan Paul.

Golberry, S. M. X. 1802. *Fragmens d'un voyage en Afrique.* Paris: Treuttel and Wurtz.

Greenberg, Joseph H. 1963. *The Languages of Africa.* The Hague: Mouton.

Haley, Alex. 1976. *Roots: The Saga of an American Family.* Garden City, N.Y.: Doubleday.

Hamlyn, W. T. 1935. *A Short Study of the Western Mandinka Language.* London: Crown Agents.

Hecquard, Hyacinte. 1855. *Voyage sur la Côte et dans l'Intérieur de l'Afrique Occidentale.* Paris: Benard.

Hopkinson, E. 1911. *Mandingo Vocabulary.* (Published with addenda in 1924.) Bathurst: Secretariat.

Jobson, Richard. 1968. *The Golden Trade.* (First published, 1623.) London: Dawsons.

Koelle, S. W. 1854. *Polyglotta Africana.* London: Church Missionary House.

Labouret, H. 1934. *Les Manding et Leur Langue.* Paris: Larousse.

Lane, Edward W. 1956. *Arabic–English Lexicon.* New York: Ungar.

Leary, Frances Anne. 1969. Islam. Politics and Colonialism: A Political History of Islam in the Casamance Region of Senegal (1850–1914). Unpublished Ph.D. thesis, Northwestern University, Evanston, Illinois.

Lévi-Strauss, Claude. 1969. *The Elementary Structures of Kinship.* (Translated and edited by Rodney Needham, with J.H. Bell and J.R. von Sturmen); London: Eyre & Spottiswoode.

Levtzion, Nehemia. 1973. *Ancient Ghana and Mali.* London: Methuen.

Lewis, B., Pellat, C., and Schacht, J. 1965. *The Encyclopedia of Islam.* London: Luzac.

Macbrair, Robert M. 1837. *A Grammar of the Mandingo Language: With Vocabularies.* London: Wesleyan Methodist Missionary Society.

Mauss, Marcel. 1969. *The Gift: Forms and Functions of Exchange in Archaic Societies.* (Translated by Ian Cunnison; first published 1925.) London: Cohen and West.

Migeod, F. W. H. 1906. *Dictionnaire Francais–Malinké et Malinké–Français.* Conakry: Mission des Pères du Saint-Esprit.

Mollien, G. 1967. *Travels in the Interior of Africa.* (First published, 1820.) London: Cass.

Moore, Francis. 1738. *Travels into Inland Parts of Africa.* London: Cave.

Needham, Rodney. 1973. Prescription. *Oceania* 43: 166–181.

———. 1974. The evolution of social classification: A commentary on the Warao case. *Bijdragen* 130: 16–43.

Norris, Edwin. 1841. *Outline of a Vocabulary of a Few of the Principal Languages of Western and Central Africa.* London: Parker.

Nunn, G. N. N. 1934. *A Short Phrase Book and Classified Vocabulary from English into Mandinka.* Bathurst: Government Printer.

Park, Mungo. 1799. *Travels in the Interior Districts of Africa.* London: Bulmer.

———. 1969. *Mungo Park's Travels in Africa.* (Reprinting the two volumes that were first published in 1799 and 1815, respectively.) London: Dent.

Pereira, Pacheco. 1937. *Esmeraldo de Situ Orbis.* (Translated and edited by G. H. T. Kimble.) London: Hakluyt Society.

Pocock, David. 1971. *Social Anthropology.* (First published 1961.) London: Sheed and Ward.

Quinn, Charlotte A. 1972. *Mandingo Kingdoms of the Senegambia.* London: Longman.

Raffenel, Anne. 1846. *Voyage dans l'Afrique occidentale, 1843–1844.* Paris: Bertrand.

Rançon, A. 1894. *Le Bondou, Étude de Géographie . . . Soudanienne de 1681 à nos Jours.* Bordeaux: Gounouilhou.

Roche, Christian. 1970. Les trois Fodé Kaba. *Notes Africaines de l'Université de Dakar et de l'IFAN* (128): 107–111.

———. 1971. Portraits des chefs Casamançais de XIXe siècle. *Revue Française d'Histoire d'Outre Mer* 58: 451–467.

———. 1972. L'Histoire oubliée de Sory Camera. *Bulletin de l'IFAN* 34: 51–66.

Rowlands, E. C. 1959. *A Grammar of Gambian Mandinka.* London: School of Oriental and African Studies.

Schaffer, Matt. 1975. Pakao Book. *African Languages/Langues Africaines* 1: 96–123.

Smith, Pierre. 1965. Les Diakhanké, histoire d'une dispersion. Notes sur l'organisation sociale des Diakhanké. *Bulletins et Mémoires de la Société d'Anthropologie de Paris* 8: 231–302.

Stanley, H. M. 1878. *Through the Dark Continent.* London: Sampson Low, Marston, Searle and Rivington.

Steinthal, H. 1867. *Die Mande–Neger–Sprachen.* Berlin: Harrowitz and Gossmann.

Stewart, F. H. 1972. Fundamentals of Age-Set Systems. Ph.D. thesis, University of Oxford.

Suárez, María Matilde. 1971. Terminology, alliance and change in Warao society. *Nieuwe West-Indische Gids* 48: 56–122.

Trimingham, J. Spencer. 1959. *Islam in West Africa.* Oxford: Clarendon Press.

Turner, Victor. 1972. *The Forest of Symbols.* Ithaca, N.Y.: Cornell University Press.

Washington, Captain. 1838. Some account of Mohammedu–Sisei, a Mandingo of Nyáni–Marú on the Gambia. *The Journal of the Royal Geographical Society of London* 8: 448–454.

Weber, Max. 1965. *The Theory of Social and Economic Organization.* (Translated by A. M. Henderson and Talcott Parsons.) New York: Free Press.

Wehr, Hans. 1971. *A Dictionary of Modern Written Arabic*. (Edited by J. Milton Cowan.) London: Allen and Unwin.

Weil, Peter M. 1971a. The masked figure and social control: The Mandinka case. *Africa* 41: 279–293.

———. 1971b. Political structure and process among the Gambia Mandinko: The village parapolitical system. In Carleton T. Hodge (ed.), *Papers on the Manding*. The Hague: Mouton, pp. 247–267.

Werner, A. 1915. *The Language Families of Africa*. London: Society for Promoting Christian Knowledge.

Wilson, J. L. 1847. Languages of Africa—Comparison between the Mandingo, Grebo and Mpongwe dialects. *Bibliotheca Sacra and Theological Review* 4: 745–772.

———. 1849. Comparative vocabularies of some of the principal Negro dialects of Africa. *Journal of the American Oriental Society* 1: 339–381.